Customizing and Tuning
MERCEDES

Customizing and Tuning
MERCEDES

Modification for Performance and Appearance

Rudolph Heitz and Thomas Neff

Motorbooks International
Publishers & Wholesalers Inc
Osceola, Wisconsin 54020, USA ®

This English language edition first published in 1988 by Motorbooks International Publishers & Wholesalers Inc, PO Box 2, 729 Prospect Avenue, Osceola, WI 54020, USA

© English language text Motorbooks International Publishers & Wholesalers Inc

First published in 1987 by Motorbuch Verlag, PO Box 1370, 7000 Stuttgart 1, West Germany

A department of the Buch- und Verlagshaus Paul Pietsch

© Motorbuch Verlag

Photographic credit: Archiv *Auto Katalog,* Autopress, many of the companies whose cars are featured in this book and the authors

Printed and bound in the United States of America

Library of Congress Cataloging-in-Publication Data

Heitz, Rudolf.
  Mercedes tuning.

  Translation of: Mercedes Tuning : Motor, Fahrwerk, Karosserie.
  Includes index.
  1. Mercedes automobile.   I. Neff, Thomas, 1947-
II. Title.
TL215.M4H4513   1987   629.28'722   87-24750
ISBN 0-87938-271-6

Contents

Preface

As early as the 1960's, the term "mass movement" found its way into the automobile manufacturer's vocabulary. Production figures rose from year to year, and an increasing number of different models appeared on the market. Competition is now becoming fiercer than ever before. But, in the final analysis, success and failure also depend to a considerable degree on customer taste and preferences. Though the philosophies of the manufacturers in the United States, Japan, Italy, France, or Germany could scarcely be more diverse, almost all of the production models that roll off their assembly lines have one thing in common—they look increasingly alike.

Even the prestigious firm of Daimler-Benz is producing an increasing number of models that look more and more like one another; and whether they belong to the so-called "compact" or middle range, or are built on a standard or long wheelbase, the 190 models are scarcely distinguishable from the 200-300 models at first glance.

Automobile tuners and stylists have long since realized this and are busily exploiting the lucrative gap that has opened up between everyday production models and the perfectly natural desire on the part of the motorist to own a car that expresses more of his own personality. And this is no bad thing, since exclusivity is as much in demand as ever, as is the joy of motoring. Even at the very top of the Daimler-Benz price range, it is no longer taboo to make mechanical and styling changes to a Mercedes.

In addition to the long-established styling companies, an unexpectedly large number of specialist firms have sprung up in Germany—in fact throughout Europe—in recent years. The old middle-range models (W 123) and the S-class models (W 126) had already aroused their interest, but it was above all the new compact 190 series (W 201) that created the additional interest in styling among the "fashion houses" of the tuning and styling world.

Unfortunately, some of these "styling artists" are too clever for their own good, but there is an old adage that there is no accounting for taste. In whatever guise, however, quality must be maintained; otherwise the customer's choice becomes not merely difficult, but positively painful. Poor workmanship has, thank heavens, a pattern of being found out sooner or later, and the market has its own way of dealing with the problem.

Visual enhancement has so far received little attention in the technical literature, since "tuning and styling" is a wide-ranging term. Basically, just about everything on a car can be enhanced—the bodywork, interior, engine, and chassis. But what is permitted, and what is not? Which companies specialize in which models? Can older models be converted as well?

This book is aimed at all Mercedes drivers, all friends of the house of Daimler-Benz, at the entire tuning and styling sector and all tuning and styling fans, as well as all those on the point of buying a prestige car with the three-pointed star on the hood.

The particular value of this book lies in the fact that it provides an insight into the wealth of possible Mercedes conversions. At the same time, it describes the many companies working in this field and gives details of their production programs. It also gives plenty of background information, practical tips, and all the relevant addresses. This reference work is concerned in particular with visual enhancements, but it also covers certain aspects of engine tuning or chassis modifications where these are of importance. It shows not only enhancements based on current Mercedes-Benz models, but also many examples of older cars that have received similar treatment. It also takes a look at the numerous compound cars based on Mercedes-Benz models, throws light on the development of styling, shows historic racing and rally models of Daimler-Benz cars, and discusses the prospects and planning for future cars from the point of view of tuning.

At the present, Daimler-Benz cars arouse far and away the greatest interest among the general public; the car with the Mercedes star on the radiator is invariably regarded as something special. Bodywork stylists, chassis specialists, and tuning experts all come forward to offer their services. Reaching for the stars will continue to be something more than just a dream.

Introduction

For many years now, consumers of industrial products have been considerably influenced by design factors. Ordinary household articles are expected to look attractive, just as expensive luxury goods are, and even quite extravagant designs will sell well. Consumers want more than just the bare functional minimum, plain and unadorned, irrespective of whether they are buying coffee grinders, telephones, stereos, or vacuum cleaners.

There can be no doubt that cars are just as much a part of the industrial design scene as consumer goods, and the shape of cars has proved to be a source of great fascination, even in their earliest days. The car offers an opportunity to express individuality and can satisfy aesthetic sensibilities. However, there can be equally little doubt that car styling represents an extremely complex and difficult area of design.

To the layman, designers and stylists are intuitively creative beings with perhaps a touch of genius, who appear to be guided only by the inspiration of the moment. But industrial car design is possible only on a teamwork basis. The common objective is to combine safety, quality, long service life, and economy with an attractive visual image.

The requirements laid down in the manufacturer's specification for a new car represent a challenge to the skill and creativity of the stylist, but at the same time they also impose limitations. The car stylist's all-too-extravagant flights of fantasy are restrained by the practical needs the car is intended to fulfill, by factors such as visibility and space, and by economic and ecological considerations, not to mention the constraints imposed by legislation. The interests of the technical, production, sales, and service departments are in constant conflict with one another, though they work closely together toward the common objective. Yet in spite of all this, the stylists manage to maintain the necessary scope for creativity.

A blending

Car manufacture is, and doubtless will always remain, a compromise. The cost-performance ratio is tailored to suit the needs of the buyer. For some, a car is merely a means to get from one place to another, whereas others expect to do the same in style and comfort. Between these two extremes there lies a world of different possibilities where individual tastes are concerned.

In the automobile industry of today, safety, economy, and environmental protection are primary considerations. Crash-tested passenger compartments provide maximum protection for the passengers and driver; headrests and seat belts reduce the risk of serious injuries; electronic devices offer protection against carelessness; computers contribute to both active and passive safety; wedge-shaped bodywork improves fuel consumption by reducing drag; and modern engines, in spite of their considerably enhanced performance, cause far less pollution than before. But the more progress is made in aerodynamics and rational design, the more these cars, all tested in the wind tunnel, tend to

9

Rear view of Mercedes 190 (W 201): production model (left) and styled version produced by MAE (right).

look alike. The natural desire for freedom of expression, self-realization, and individuality is increasingly pushed to one side.

The gap between the mass-produced output of the volume car manufacturer and the individual creation that would fulfill man's desire for self-expression is now almost as wide as the range of different possibilities now open to the motorist seeking a measure of exclusivity. Styling companies offer everything that is beautiful and expensive, from racing car look-alikes to exotic dream cars. Individuality is "in," and exclusivity is the key. Car stylists are having a field day—at least, until the money runs out.

Established firms of stylists advertise their products in their own special expensively produced catalogs; the "formula for better motoring, increased safety, greater comfort, and enhanced technology" is trumpeted from the pages of composite brochures. By use of chassis kits, wide tires, light-alloy wheels, aerodynamic body parts, sport steering wheels and seats, as well as styled interiors, any standard production model can be converted into something highly individual. The possibilities for styling are simply endless, and as we have already said, there is no accounting for taste.

The problems only arise when it comes to deciding which of all the firms in the German tuning and styling fraternity is the best. Personal opinions and philosophies in this respect are as many and varied as the creations of the individual "fashion houses" themselves. But in one respect, at least, they are in complete agreement—the managers of the various tuning and styling companies all emphasize the seriousness of their commitment and the special attraction of individually converting and enhancing production car models.

A number of factors appear to fly in the face of reason or, in this case, technology itself—and more specifically, vehicle technology.

Pictures of mass-produced cars from the volume car manufacturers already show an astonishing degree of similarity in styling, for the knowledge and experience gained in wind tun-

Mercedes Research car 2000. Favorable drag, high level of safety, and lightweight construction are the bodywork characteristics. The coefficient of drag is under 0.3.

nel testing all point in one direction, to result in a single wind-cheating variant. All that remains then is stylistic retouching to make the individual marques more easily identifiable. No doubt, the addition of some further desirable instruments and controls, and interiors based on meticulous research prompted by the motoring public at large, will increase the degree of differentiation; but in this area, too, an increasing measure of uniformity is becoming apparent.

Somewhere here—where technology and progress blend with futuristic concepts to take absolute form and go into production as "proven miracles"—styling comes onto the scene and in its own way also imposes restraints. If an individual seeks to put his very own personal philosophy into action, then his faith in technology and progress can work with it to enhance the quality of life. The way is opened up for creative development; something of the ego of the individual is given external expression. Obstinate individualism? Perhaps, but heaven preserve us from a

uniform future that leaves no room for dreams and fun.

The special attraction of this sector is to be found in the trade as a whole, in individualism and in the individual people, in the challenge to oneself and in the creation and refining of something special—in short, in styling. It would certainly be wrong to think of it only on a grand scale. It would also certainly be wrong to turn up one's nose too often. In the styling business, the crosscurrents of tradition, aesthetics, sports, and individualism are woven together into a rich tapestry. This has now taken on a relatively concrete form and been reduced to a common denominator—automobile styling and tuning. There is a lot of very hard work involved, but there are countless anecdotes to tell: the arguments with clients who are continually changing their ideas, usually when the work is almost completed; the meek and the mighty who express their wishes in a whisper or a roar; the well-known public figures who do not wish to be

Indy 500, an extreme example of a converted Mercedes by Benny S-Car, based on the SEC 500. Conversion costs approximately 40,000 marks, red leather interior 20,000 marks, sports dashboard 5,000 marks, side-mounted exhaust system 5,000 marks; special items such as stereo equipment and engine tuning on request.

named, but nevertheless love to pose in front of their dream cars . . . and many more besides.

The enormous versatility of this particular sector ensures that nothing ever comes to a stop, or ever will. The orders pour in, and the appeal of innovation is a constant, deliberate, and creative cycle. It calls for a great deal of enthusiasm on the part of the customer and, naturally, also on the part of the stylist. Some people collect stamps, others love to travel, and others again are fond of good food and wines; but there is one thing common to all customers and stylists—their love for a very special car.

Glitter and glory are certainly often associated with dreams and wishes, with that little bit extra to the quality of life and the personal touch. Fired with enthusiasm by endless lists of extras available from the manufacturer, and seduced by the beautiful special products offered by the stylists, the customer of today can easily put together a car that precisely matches his own idea—his dream car. He also has the feeling of

having contributed to the design, since he can select each special item himself. And why not? This image of perfection is backed up by technical know-how and first-class workmanship.

So it is not just a dream after all? Perhaps it is a matter of realistic wishes and desires, the pleasure and fulfillment of one of the visible status symbols of our time.

Hans-Albert Zender, the stylist from Mulheim, refers, for example, to the main body of car buyers when he writes in the foreword to the annual *Zender Catalogue:* "For some people, a car is a pleasant but nonetheless utilitarian item of everyday use, like a spin dryer or a coffee making machine—four wheels which take him about his daily business, the purchase of which is governed almost exclusively by economic criteria. A point of view which one can fully understand! But then there are 'us' and 'them.' We are people who are enthusiastic about cars; we also want to travel from one place to another, but in a very special way. We want to change the appear-

Drawing of a Mercedes 500 converted into a station wagon, as styled by Zender.

ance of a particular production car model slightly, to give it our own particular style. It we really want to translate this desire into reality, then the most fantastic possibilities are opened up."

The cost

Although this book deals only with Mercedes conversions, it is astonishing how the number of stylists has risen in recent years. *Auto Motor und Sport* (Vol. 14/1985) spoke recently of Mercedes as the "Number 1 in the styling business." Even Federal Chancellor Konrad Adenauer drove a modified Mercedes. He had all the ashtrays removed from his Mercedes 300 and had the gaps carefully covered over. Daimler-Benz charged him the symbolic fee of 25 marks! It would probably cost a bit more than that today. Rapidly increasing turnover has made styling Mercedes cars into Germany's secret growth industry, one that profits from one of the enviable traits of the typical Mercedes owner, namely, that he is accustomed to putting quality before price. Such people are prepared to pay more to have their cars made more individual.

Conversion of a Mercedes 190 costs, as a rule, between 4,000 and 12,000 marks. If the car is an S-class model, then the potential customer would have to be prepared to put down an additional 20,000 to 30,000 marks, on top of the approximately 90,000 marks price tag on a fully equipped Mercedes 500 SEL. (In summer of 1987, one mark was valued at approximately fifty-four cents.)

Naturally, there is no upper limit to the costs. The "couturiers and cosmetic artists" among the styling and tuning fraternity can offer a special type of custom collection for those who are prepared to pay up to 500,000 marks or more.

Admittedly, some manufacturers found themselves in a terrible financial squeeze as a result of pursuing the wrong product policy and losing their markets to the oil-producing countries and in the United States. In some cases, the quality of the conversions left a great deal to be desired, even to the point of irresponsibility. In such cases of mismanagement, one can only be glad that the market has its own way of ridding itself of such unwelcome operators.

Quality and safety must be the most important priorities, and conversion at all cost is an entirely misconceived and reprehensible approach. This has nothing to do with converting, modifying, and generally rebuilding an S-class Mercedes, so as to be able to claim it as the one and only example of its type in the world.

This is where the technical qualifications of the styling company play a decisive role. So is it to be "haute couture" in car manufacturing, or just styling pure and simple? Specialists who call themselve stylists or tuners see ever-increasing possibilities for innovative and creative self-development in the optimization and aesthetics of car conversions. In some cases, this can lead them to the very limit of what is technically justifiable, creating special tasks and making the very highest demands on their skills—tasks that are carried out at enormous cost and effort and take into account all the special characteristics of a car. Car styling and tuning is an amalgam of technical tuning and visual enhancement, including the interior and special modifications to the bodywork, with the various changes becoming an integral whole, no longer visible as separate entities. The various disciplines involved can scarcely be separated. Every conceivable thread is brought together, with the simplest and the most unusual requests and individual characteristics—and it is very rare for the one not to interact with the other. The resulting alternatives and variants, and the expansion into almost all areas of modification and conversion, are what the tuners and stylists really want. And these demands bring out the skill and precision and the design abilities of each individual entrepreneur.

The expression coined by the leading stylists ABC, of Bonn, "haute couture in the car industry," is somehow the most apt name for this sector. The French term is entirely appropriate and reflects the quality of the product with regard to both the interior and the exterior.

And even if there are a few black sheep, the sector in which a sort of traditional craftsman's guild has sprung up—and not without good reason—will maintain its position as a result of the efforts of its best proponents. In this guild, old crafts that would scarcely have enjoyed any sort of future at all in any other context have found new life. Engineers, upholsterers, saddlers, coachbuilders, model makers, and designers have found new challenges and new outlets for their skills with the styling companies in tasks that fascinate the specialist, especially the young one. Anyone who has ever got involved with "passion wagons," as the stylized models produced by Hans-Werner Aufrecht, the head of AMG in Affalterbach in Swabia, are called, will scarcely be able to tear himself away again and will apply quite different standards to himself and his work thereafter. Perfection, the ultimate in safety, creativity, and the very highest skills must not be allowed to become debased through familiarity but must continue to play an essential role in this trade and all its branches. A love of detail and an incurable weakness for cars are the best qualifications.

But all this does not spring up out of nothing and should not be seen as self-evident; it also requires huge amounts of money, quite apart from a great deal of extremely hard and dedicated work. Aufrecht, the owner of AMG, is prepared to put a figure of approximately one million marks on the development costs for an average series of models, excluding tooling—250,000 and 500,000 marks, respectively, for the external styling and engine, and about 250,000 for the chassis.

A simple calculation, broken down into its constituent parts, will illustrate the enormous expense involved in a single program. At the same time, it will serve to point up the huge number of factors that have to be considered. A current model, the Mercedes 200-300 E (W 124), will be used as an example.

The lowest level of styling worth considering exists in the development of a set of body styling parts. The standard version, that is, the production model without any modifications to the existing paneling or chassis, consists of front, spoiler, rocker panels, and rear apron.

Nowdays, the following are almost obligatory: SEC-styled hood, and modified trunk lid or top-mounted foil.

Development of these parts to the point where they can be sold involves the following stages:

• design sketches,

- studies on reduced-scale models or rough modeling on a full-sized vehicle,
- development of prototype on a vehicle,
- testing of prototype by Technical Control Board (TUV), with respect to downpressure and brake cooling,
- detailed development of prototype,
- model finishing, ready to make preliminary molds,
- production of a prototype part in glass-fiber-reinforced plastic (GRP),
- final detailed fitting of prototype part on vehicle, with all fastenings and accessory parts,
- final acceptance by TUV of prototype part made from GRP, with test certification of the material,
- production of final working molds for GRP parts.

If production of the spoiler parts is included in series production from hard plastic foam, then foam molds must also be produced.

If a small set of parts is to be developed professionally, then a rough figure of between 10,000 and 25,000 marks per part must be reckoned with, so that the development costs for the simplest possible set, consisting of front spoiler, rocker panels, and rear apron, would run between 40,000 and 75,000 marks. To this must be added the relevant sums for rear foils or trunk lid and hood.

These are the costs involved if the parts in question are handmade using GRP molds. If the same parts are pressed from the same materials, or made from foam, then the costs for each part would be increased by several thousand marks for tooling costs. The pressing mold for a front spoiler of GRP, for example, would be in the region of 15,000 to 30,000 marks, and the foam molds for the same part would be between 40,000 and 150,000 marks.

These sums of money—which constitute an investment—can only be amortized if sales are sufficiently high, and they are accordingly apportioned by the manufacturers of the parts to orders of a given size, perhaps one hundred or one thousand. The stylists manufacture the parts themselves only in the rarest cases.

If, in addition to the standard version, there is to be a wide version, involving sizable modifications, then the costs can be doubled again.

If fenders are widened, then another 20,000 marks can be added by the time they are ready for production.

If the chassis is to be fitted with wide wheels and tires that have already been approved by the TUV, then between 15,000 and 50,000 can be added to the bill, depending on how much the planned dimensions deviate from the standard version. If, for example, 225/50 tires are requested instead of the 195/60 tires fitted to the standard version, then the costs of testing are relatively low and, apart from a few thousand kilometers of test driving on the Hockenheimring, will be mostly restricted to ensuring the necessary clearance in the fenders. However, if 285/40 or 345/35 tires are used on correspondingly large wheels, then the strength of the wheel suspensions, the rigidity of the bodywork in the suspension areas, and a number of other factors have to be tested as well.

In most cases, the use of such extreme tire sizes would affect the driving characteristics of the car to such an extent that long and expensive test drives would be required to achieve an acceptable compromise between ride comfort, driving characteristics, hydroplaning behavior, active and passive safety, and the desired styling.

It is therefore astonishing that the TUV should have been prepared to approve the use on middle-range cars like the Mercedes 190 or 3-series BMW of wide tires of sizes such as 225/50 or even 245/45 at the front and 285/40 or 345/35 at the rear. It is scarcely imaginable that this can be justified with a clear conscience, if only because of the extreme danger of hydroplaning with such tires on comparatively light cars.

If steering characteristics are seriously affected by negative changes to the suspension geometry and by drastically increased forces transmitted to the wheel and suspension mountings on the bodywork, then there will always be a considerable deterioration in service life and operating characteristics, which will be absolutely on the limit of what is justifiable with regard to safety and certification.

It was not all that long ago that things were

15

very different. Where cars were concerned, exclusivity consisted in owning a car—not infrequently handmade—of one of the exotic luxury marques, mostly British, French, or Italian, which nowadays unfortunately have mostly disappeared from the scene. But the present-day tuning and styling trend has one undeniable advantage: With most of the representatives of this fraternity, the technical side of their operations is kept within limits that are easily supervised, so that sacrifices in serviceability or reliability rarely, if ever, have to be made.

Furthermore, many companies that have built up a good reputation in this field over many years can still boast continuing success in the field of motor sport, and in most cases have long years of experience in the technical enhancement of production car models. Skilled craftsmanship and a wealth of innovations on the part of the specialists have helped German tuners and stylists to achieve worldwide acclaim and recognition.

Styling evolution

Whether body styling makes sense is answered clearly by the many customers. The car with an individual style, the personal touch, self-realization, the desire to set oneself apart from the masses—all these are in vogue. The owner of a car enhanced through additional styling is, in the final analysis, trying to display his own individuality.

Body styling, that is, the later addition of styling features to a standard production model, started in its widest sense at the beginning of the 1950's, when the Wiesbaden-based firm of Kamei fitted a so-called deep control to the legendary VW Beetle. The result of this attempt to give the popular Beetle a front spoiler was a sharp-edge sheet-metal attachment fitted beneath the front bumper.

Today one can only smile at such rudimentary and unsophisticated attempts at enhancement, especially since the "snowplow" as it came to be popularly known in do-it-yourself (DIY) circles, would no longer pass muster with the Technical Control Board. For many years now, the trend of enhancements has been toward complete all-round kits that not only enhance the appearance of the car but also improve its performance. Exclusivity and a sporting look are much in demand, coupled with improved road holding, increased stability in crosswind conditions, a lower coefficient of drag, and lower fuel consumption.

Body styling is today the central feature of car modification and conversion. "Tweaking" engines and lowering chassis—which is where it all began in the 1950's and 1960's—nowadays accounts for only a fraction of the market for the tuning and styling fraternity. The majority of styling artists restrict themselves exclusively to visual enhancements. A small number of firms specialize in certain marques. For example, AMG in Affalterbach and Lorinser in Waiblingen concentrate exclusively on Daimler-Benz products from the factory in Stuttgart-Unterturkheim.

The repertoire of conversions includes front and rear spoilers, rocker panels, rear aprons, and extended fenders, among other parts; it also includes installation of expensive audio and video equipment and exclusive styling of the interior. Standard limousines are made into convertibles and notchback limousines into coupes. "Stretched" and armor-plated coachwork also figure among the special commissions received. Finally, there are extreme degrees of styling produced for shows, which account for some strange excrescences and gaudy coachwork.

Is extra styling really necessary? Of course, one can easily do without such enhancements, as one can do without many other consumer goods. But in these times of high living standards, where everyone is consumer-oriented and where society is relatively secure, an ever-increasing percentage of the population feels the need to express individuality and to raise themselves above the broad mass of the population. How better to do that than by owning a prestigious car? The appearance of the car can reflect its owner's exclusive personality and individuality, especially with the marked increase in the number of parts fitted to improve the aerodynamic characteristics of cars in the middle range.

The modern production car fulfills most expectations so far as performance is concerned, so the majority of customers—and no longer only the male ones—tend to go for styling and to leave the engine and chassis in original condition. They want the car at their front door to be their very own car, with all that this implies.

Earlier generations of spoilers were purely functional in design, and reminded one of nothing so much as racing car accessories. Early attempts at enhancement have long since been overtaken by developments in aerodynamics and styling in car manufacture. Body conversion parts may no longer be attached to production models purely for their visual effect, but must also be designed in accordance with sound technological principles. In this respect, even the most simple considerations can play a very important role. For example, the rear apron also fulfills the role of a conventional fender flap. Every part must comply with the statutory regu-

The Mercedes 190 (W 201) series covers an output range that extends from the 53 kW (72 hp) diesel engine to the 136 kW (185 hp) sixteen-valve unit. The reliability of this series has long since become a matter of record, whether in the world record runs in Nardo (top left) or during the official opening race on the Nurburgring (bottom left).

Front spoiler and rocker panel by Lorinser.

lations laid down for testing by the Type Testing Center of the TUV.

The body parts designed for attaching to production models can basically be broken down into groups: front spoilers, rocker panels, widened fenders, rear aprons, rear spoilers and foils, radiator grilles.

In addition, a number of relatively minor parts, for example, wind splits, hood trim, roof spoilers and foils, and racing mirrors, are available.

Although the emphasis continues to be on front and rear spoilers, there have been considerable changes of emphasis. The automobile industry has taken advantage of the work done by the stylists in conditioning the market and is now offering a number of these enhancements, either as standard features or as extras, for a variety of models straight from the factory.

Not long ago, front and rear spoilers accounted for a considerable proportion of the turnover of the styling firms. These same firms are now designing complete conversion kits, including rocker panels and rear aprons. But the manufacturers are moving in this direction too,

Rear foil and apron by AMG.

Luxurious interior, custom made by Trasco.

slowly perhaps, but nonetheless visibly. They are profiting from the pioneering work carried out by the styling firms and are now offering styling enhancements consisting of spoilers and extended fenders, either directly as extras or on special models. Well-known show stylists are even cooperating closely with the manufacturers.

On the other hand, the manufacturers of production cars can no longer dispense with the glamorous image of special models. The volume car producers are looking to improve their sales by offering everyday models with visual enhancements; with the up-market producers of famous marques, such as Mercedes-Benz and

BMW, exclusive show cars of superlative quality are more a sign of good breeding.

The pressure of competition can lead to imitation. Everyone looks around to see what the others are up to and every company has produced its own version. In the case of BMW, the M-models are produced. Among the cars produced in Stuttgart with the three-pointed star, the Mercedes 190 E2.3-16 from the W 201 series is the first Mercedes car deliberately designed with visual and mechanical refinements in mind—the top model and at the same time the image-maker of a series that has yet to pass the test of the market.

Chapter 1

Aerodynamics

The wind plays its part in shaping the cars of the future. Will the cars of the future all look alike? Will aerodynamics, as an essential aid to reducing fuel consumption, for example, result in a more uniform, standard shape? This has long been a subject of lively discussion and widespread anxiety among the volume car manufacturers. The many customers who favor tuners and stylists have long since delivered their verdict through the interest they have shown in individually styled and modified cars. They wish to distance themselves from the uniformity of mass-produced cars.

Naturally, customer preferences will also influence the design objectives of the automobile industry. But not all of these wishes can be fully realized. The car undergoing development must offer a compromise between price and performance. If money is no object, of course, just about anything is possible, but it may not be marketable. This is where the producers of luxury cars with a personal touch have an easier time; they can devote themselves totally to fulfilling the individual wishes of their clients, while the volume car manufacturer must always have regard to the purses and the wishes of the broader masses.

Every stylist tries to produce an attractive product. An automobile designer cannot, however, be concerned merely with elegant coachwork and lavish interiors, but must also take into account a whole host of other factors that at first sight appear to be at odds with one another. For example, a family car should primarily be comfortable, practical, and safe. These characteristics will determine its final shape and appearance. The designer must also come up with a style that will give the finished car its own separate identity.

More than ever before, streamlining the bodywork is of prime importance when designing a new car. Sharp edges and protrusions cause turbulence, which reduces performance and increases fuel consumption. At speeds as low as 60 km/h, more power is required to overcome wind resistance than to make up for the mechanical losses in the power unit and the tires. Tests with cars in the same size and performance categories have shown that a reduction of the drag coefficient from 0.5 to 0.4 can reduce the fuel consumption by ten percent. The drag coefficient has become, as it were, a mark of quality where the shape of a car is concerned.

However, it is not only the wind resistance as measured in the direction of travel that plays an important part. Buffeting from crosswinds can also have an adverse effect on the running characteristics and the directional constraint of a car. And at high speed, the streams of air passing over the bodywork can have a not inconsiderable suction effect on the rear wheels, thereby reducing road-holding. If a car is to maintain its line at high speed and in difficult crosswinds, then the wheels must be sufficiently loaded to keep them firmly on the road. Designers are therefore forced to seek the best possible compromise between wind resistance and lift.

Whereas in the past, any streamlining measures were not even started until the actual design work was completed, present-day designers and aerodynamicists work closely together to find the optimum shape for the specification, in the interests of both the appearance of the car and wind resistance.

The study of aerodynamics is nothing new, and even Leonardo da Vinci grappled with aerodynamic problems in his attempts to design a flying machine. Where the car is concerned, investigations into airflow only began to attract attention when the first really fast cars were developed. While Gottlieb Daimler and Carl Benz could build cars largely as they thought fit and to suit their own taste in styling, the aerodynamics expert of today plays a very important role in the designing of a car. And with good reason, too: Fuel consumption, deflection of road dirt, susceptibility to crosswinds, and lift all have a causal connection to the problems of aerodynamics.

Just how hard air can be, and how powerful, quickly becomes clear when high winds with strengths of 6 to 8 or even gale-force 12, batter doors and windows, rip off roofs, and uproot sturdy trees. Forces of this order of magnitude confront every car while it is traveling—the only difference being, of course, that the car for the most part generates this wind resistance as a result of its speed. In order to be able to overcome this wind resistance, or drag as it is known, power is required. The less power an engine needs for this purpose, the lower its fuel consumption and its running costs.

There is a large measure of agreement in the automobile industry today that the era of "cheap aerodynamics" is now over. In the future no appreciable progress can be made in that direction with nothing more to go on than clever ideas, a measure of intuition, and detailed design work of a largely empirical nature. Instead, we are on the threshold of an era of "expensive aerodynamics," in which even the smallest step forward will require major investment in research and computing. Further insight into the complex processes of airflow becomes increasingly difficult the more our knowledge deepens. Occasionally, conflicts arise out of the needs of competing technologies—for example, between the size of engines and their cooling-air requirements. Further reductions in wind resistance call for expensive detail work, such as enclosing the irregular undersurfaces of the car, possibly with an integrated air duct to cool the exhaust system.

The effect of adding bodywork parts to production cars is likewise a complicated issue, since they serve to enhance the appearance of the car but the altered design has certain technological benefits as well. They are subject to certain statutory regulations. Special attention must be paid to dynamic values, namely, the behavior of the car while in motion, to statics, to certain safety factors, and to thermal behavior.

So far as dynamic values are concerned, the so-called C_d value, lift and downpressure, and changes in the cross section of the vehicle surface over which the air flows are decisive. The statical values include the external dimensions of add-on parts, the enclosing of the running surfaces of the tires, the overhang at each end of the bodywork, and, for example, the ground clearance. Safety factors chiefly relate to materials and accident safety. Finally, with regard to thermal behavior, the cooling of the brakes is of particular importance.

The question of improving the C_d value crops up time and again when styling is discussed. Let us therefore start by explaining the significance of the C_d value and how it is measured.

Since the earliest days of the motor car, designers have sought to improve the shape of cars in order to reduce the drag. Theoretically speaking, the ideal shape for minimum resistance is the droplet. This has always been seen in the automobile industry, as elsewhere, as the non plus ultra. Nowadays, however, in car construction the wedge shape is considered to be the most acceptable variant, similar to a droplet cut in half and with its tail truncated. Wind tunnels, the modern equivalent of the old wind machine, make it possible to optimize this shape. There is nothing new in this, since Professor Ferdinand Porsche made constant use of wind tunnel experiments in developing the VW Beetle—and that was back in the 1930's.

The function of the wind tunnel is easy

This streamlined 2.5-liter Formula 1 racing car (W 196)
of 1954, was tested in the experimental wind tunnel in
Stuttgart. Technical details: eight-cylinder engine of
2.5-liter capacity, 260–280 hp at 8500 rpm.

enough to explain: A stream of air is directed at the vehicle with varying degrees of force. Electronic measuring devices record the effects of the airstream on the vehicle. Experiments with a life-size car actually represent the second stage of the process; the first is carried out on small models, usually built to a scale of 1:5, in a correspondingly smaller wind tunnel.

In order to be able to measure the coefficient of drag, which has no dimension, testers place the vehicle with all four wheels on a form of weighbridge that records all the forces acting on the car as a result of the wind. The forces acting on each wheel are measured, as well as the lateral forces and the drag.

The C_d value is the coefficient of drag. This is merely a variable that permits comparisons to be made with other bodies and shapes, such as a droplet, a sphere, or a disk. Initially, the size or

Daimler-Benz wind tunnel. The blower orifice resembles a giant mouth. This is where car shapes are streamlined.

shape of the object is not taken into consideration.

The true or specific value for drag is therefore made up of the coefficient of drag, C_d, and the cross-sectional area, A, of an object, for example, a car. The formula $C_d \times A$ gives the drag. In practice—and even more so in theory—the speed of airflow, the air density, and the back pressure all play a role as well.

The value computed from these variables makes it possible to compare the absolute values of the forces required to move two different cars against the wind at a certain speed. This value is used to express the aerodynamic efficiency of a car. The lower the C_d value, the lower the drag as compared with other cars of comparable size and the lower the power required by the engine to overcome it—and, accordingly, the lower the fuel consumption. Today it is not only the prices, appearances, colors, and engine performances that are compared with one another—the C_d value is now of equal importance.

In this respect—superficially, at any rate—there is a contradiction in most styling measures:

A new shape in the making. Clay models are produced on a scale of 1:5, based on initial drawings. These models already show the basic characteristics of the final shape of the new car (top). The models whose shapes hold out the best possibilities for further development are then selected (middle).

Whether the model is built on a scale of 1:5 or 1:1, it is tested in the wind tunnel to determine its aerodynamic characteristics in order to be able to make the detail changes that will result in the most favorable coefficient of drag. The smoke trails enable the test engineer to see how the airflow follows the outline of the front and rear ends.

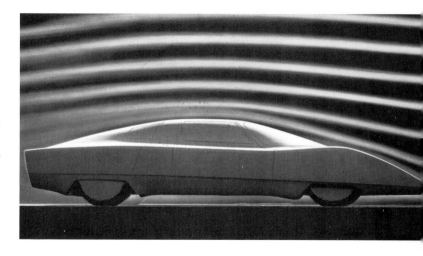

The cross-sectional area presented to the wind is actually increased by the addition of accessories and wider wheels and tires.

For example, with the addition of a spoiler, the C_d value can be improved by five percent. But this positive effect can easily be completely negated by the increased cross-sectional area. There are more than enough examples of this in practice. The decisive question is therefore more of a philosophical nature and must be answered by each individual in the light of personal requirements: Does the driver want the car to look broad and powerful, and be a little slower in the straight but usually a little faster in cornering, or want it to be rather slower in the cornering, with some sacrifice of good looks, but to reach higher speeds in the straight?

Distribution of pressure over front and rear ends.

Distribution of pressure over front and rear ends

Lift and downpressure on the Mercedes 190 E (top) and 190 E 2.3-16. The rear spoiler reduces the front axle lift by 57 percent and the C_d value by four percent; the rear spoiler and apron have a similar effect on the rear end (ΔC_d –3%, ΔAH –40%).
C_p = coefficient of pressure (C_d)

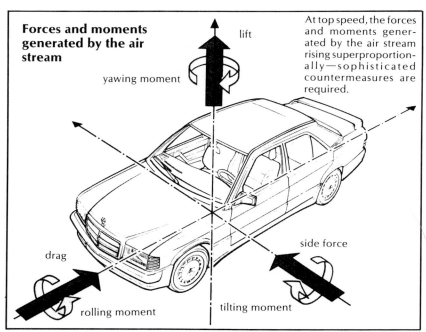

At top speed, the forces and moments generated by the air stream rising superproportionally—sophisticated countermeasures are required.

Forces and moments generated by airflow.

Mercedes 190 E 2.3-16: The large front spoiler of this 16-valve car reduces front axle lift by 57 percent and improves the C_d value by four percent, as compared with the normal 190 model.

The more a car hugs the road at high speed, the better are its straight-line and cornering characteristics and speeds. These features are particularly appreciated by motorists of the sporting type. These are the very drivers who are principally interested in spoilers. These reduce lift, and can even contribute to downpressure. Racing drivers have been exploiting this effect for many years, particularly since the real fireballs among today's racing cars can reach higher speeds on the track than a jet on takeoff. The aerodynamic shape of the racing car is specially designed to apply the right amount of pressure to press it down firmly on the track.

Aerodynamic considerations are, of course, equally valid for fast everyday cars, but only if the shape and design of the aerodynamic parts have been computed with the aid of a wind tunnel.

Many an apron of sheet metal or plastic attached by a DIY enthusiast falls foul of curbs, the vehicle registration laws, and, last but by no means least, the basic principles of aerodynamics.

The air dam under the front bumper, for instance, should always serve two purposes: to reduce the drag and to cut down the lift. In some cases, however, a spoiler must also ensure that an adequate amount of air is directed onto the front wheel brakes. Even quite small spoilers can fulfill these requirements. The bigger and deeper they are, the greater their effect—but in the case of everyday cars, there is, of course, a limit.

The complete and ideal solution to the aerodynamic problems of the car is simply not possible, on account of all the practical requirements (the specification, customer wishes, commercial considerations). In practice, the manufacturer seeks to get as close as possible to the ideal solution by means of breakaway edges at the rear of the car, which is quite high anyway, smoother underbodies, glued-on window frames, concealed windshield wipers, sharply angled front, rear, and side windows, and so on.

Reduction of drag has been shown to be an effective means of improving the economy of cars. But aerodynamic shapes are increasingly creating new problems of their own, for instance, with regard to the characteristic curves of engines, the tuning of drives, and the channeling of air to the cooling system and the interior of the car. Windshields and rear windows set at a shallow angle result in increased temperatures inside the car when the sun is shining, while visibility, especially to the rear, can suffer as a result of the optimized exterior shape.

The styling artists naturally put forward their own point of view, while the technical experts insist that their approach to the realization of aerodynamic objectives is the right one. The golden mean probably lies in reaching the best possible compromise for everyday motoring— and that is normally somewhere in the middle.

They all do have one thing in common: Development today involves testing in a wind tunnel. This means that the C_d value will level out. A few years ago, the average value for a passenger car was 0.44. Today, values of 0.29 to 0.35, with a slight reduction in the cross-sectional area, are by no means rare within just one generation of models. In the case of the Mercedes 190/190 E (W 201), the C_d is, for example, 0.33; it is 0.3 for the 200-300 E (W 124) and about 0.27 for the new SL roadster, which will appear from 1987-88 onward. The same excellent value can also be expected from the next S-class generation (from 1990-91).

World record holder La Vettura: The record was set on April 29, 1899, in Acheres, France, when a speed of 105.88 km/h was achieved. Driver: Camillo Jenatzy.

Chapter 2

Registration regulations

It is an old saying that the devil takes refuge in detail. And since the Vehicle Registration Regulations (StVZO) are full of pitfalls for the unwary, many motorists bent on enhancing their beloved cars can all too easily find themselves in conflict with the regulations.

Within the purview of the Vehicle Registration Regulations (StVZO), all the important parts of a car have to undergo a special test procedure. This is carried out by the TUV and the Federal Office of Motor Transport (KBA). All parts tested and found to be acceptable are assigned a test number, or a Design Assessment is drawn up. This applies to both standard production components and accessories.

ABE and ABG procedures

Before a production car is allowed out on the road, the manufacturer must obtain a General License to Operate (ABE), in which the state of the car as it leaves the production line is described in great detail. This does not mean that the subsequent owner may not modify the vehicle at all. Provided that one does not replace or modify any of the vital parts of the car, one can do pretty much as one pleases: paint it any color (though fluorescent paint is forbidden!), carpet the floor, put covers on the seats, install a radio, and even remove the bumpers (including their mountings, of course). Provided that none of these enhancements affects the fundamental safety of the car in any way, either internally or externally, then there is nothing to stop an owner from making changes.

However, if any vital parts of the car are replaced or modified in any way, then great care is needed. The law makes specific provisions regarding many of the parts of a car, such as the lighting system, windows, and tow bars, and these require a General Design Approval (ABG).

With other important parts, the law lays down a specific safety standard. Parts covered in this way include braking and steering systems, steering wheels, rims, tires, parts of the chassis, glass roof panels, exhaust units, and spoilers.

The accessory shops are full to overflowing with accessories of this sort; one can buy them anywhere, but actually installing or attaching them may be an entirely different matter. In order to be absolutely certain where one stands, one should buy only parts that come with a test certificate from the TUV or have a General License to Operate (ABE). This will state whether the part is suitable for the vehicle in question, what one should look out for when installing or attaching it, and whether it needs to be approved once installed, in accordance with section 19 of the Vehicle Registration Regulations—that is, whether one should drive the car straight round to the experts at the local TUV office.

But there is one thing common to all parts that have the blessing of an ABE or an ABG—once they have been installed or attached, the General License to Operate of the vehicle itself may become invalid. If this happens, then an expert from the TUV would have to confirm with a signature that the part has been properly installed, and at the same time check whether the part is approved for use on that particular type of vehicle. After that, there is the little matter of a visit to the Vehicle Licensing Office, where the vehicle papers are amended.

If nonapproved parts are used, the design approval, and with it the vehicle's General License to Operate, automatically becomes invalid. If police checks should be carried out, the owner of such a car can look forward to a summons, a fine, and the loss of a few points in his license. If the officials dealing with the case are particularly strict, the car could be ordered off the road immediately.

If there is no obligatory visit to the TUV laid down for parts that have a General License to Operate, then the ABE document must always be kept on hand, preferably in the glove compartment. If the police should check the car for any reason, they may ask to see it.

Before buying such a part, or at least before installing or attaching it, the car owner should be well advised to obtain the relevant information in order to avoid any unpleasant surprises, especially since there is an enormous range of different possibilities between what is always permitted and what is strictly forbidden:

- Purely decorative items such as trim or rubber bumpers have absolutely no bearing whatsoever on the General License to Operate, provided that they are securely mounted and not liable to cause injury
- Spoilers, wide wheels, and steering wheels should always have a General License to Operate, valid for the type of car in question, or a Design Assessment
- If a so-called installation inspection and acceptance is required for a particular accessory, then the TUV must confirm that it has been correctly installed or attached
- If extras are sold with the TUV Design Assessment, then after the parts have been correctly installed or attached, the car must be taken to the appropriate officials to have the new parts inspected and entered in the vehicle papers; all the other essential conditions relating to the installation or attachment—some of which involve considerable expense—must also be fulfilled

- Parts that have neither an ABE nor a Design Assessment are subject to particularly strict checks; the chances of getting them approved will be better if the vehicle manufacturer has issued a Clearance Certificate, but this is extremely unlikely for parts that do not already have an ABE

Naturally, any owner who carries out special conversions or modifications to a car is free to turn to the TUV of his own accord, but an inspection is quite time-consuming and relatively expensive. It could cost a few hundred to a few thousand marks, depending on the part in question. The acceptance costs for a front spoiler, with just a single road trial, can run to between 1500 and 5000 marks. And these are just the TUV's costs, not including the price of the models, molds, or parts.

Anyone who still ventures out on the road with forbidden accessories can expect serious trouble in the event of being involved in an accident. If the forbidden part is responsible for the accident, then the unfortunate victim's damages will be covered by the third-party insurance, but the insurance company could seek recourse from the owner of the car responsible— even with fully comprehensive insurance. It would be sheer madness if every single new car had to be presented for inspection by the Vehicle Test Centers. The manufacturer therefore obtains a General License to Operate for Vehicle Types (ABE) for each of its models before series production commences. This ABE automatically covers each and every one of the cars of this model produced to a precisely defined design and equipment specification. It contains details of all the parts variants available from the manufacturer and approved by the TUV, for instance, the types and sizes of tires approved by the manufacturer. In most cases, the owner can check up on these in the vehicle log. For example, it might say "Size of tires: 195/60 VR 14," and under the heading of comments, "Also approved: 175/70 VR 14." This means that both sizes of tire are tested and approved. Any other size would have to be approved and entered by the TUV in the vehicle papers; otherwise there could be serious trouble for the owner in the event of a police check.

The amount of work involved in testing is enormous. Here is a small and by no means comprehensive selection from the tests involved: Are the frame and steering system sufficiently strong and resistant to distortion? Are there any dangerous corners or edges anywhere on the bodywork or any projecting pieces of metal? Is the tank sturdy enough and installed in a safe place? Are the headlamps of an approved type and mounted in the prescribed position? Are the rear lights set at the correct height and are the side clearances correct? Is the exhaust system correctly suspended and efficient, and are the noxious substances in the exhaust gases within the legal limits? What is the engine performance like? Are the permissible sound intensity limits being exceeded? Are the brakes adequate for the weight and possible speed of the car, and are they subject to fade with heavy use? Are the seats and safety belts securely anchored? And on a more general level: Is the behavior of the car satisfactory, even on bad roads and at high speeds? Does any body rock occur, or any pitching, yawing, or rolling?

In order to have all that checked, and much more besides, the factory must provide the TUV or some other authorized body with specimens of the vehicle type in question in all its variations (for example, with the different types of tire, versions of the engine, and transmission) so that these authorities can carry out the necessary tests on behalf of the Federal Office of Motor Transport (KBA) in Flensburg.

Often enough, however, the manufacturer is unable to provide a complete model of the car because development work is still in progress. Perhaps the headlamps envisaged are not available yet, or the bumpers are not available in their final form, or the exhaust system is only a temporary one. So the new model is tested in stages. In this way, although the individual tests could take up only a few weeks in total, the overall process may be spread over more than six months from commencement of testing to issuing the ABE.

EC and ECE

A new model is tested not only in accordance with the Vehicle Registration Regulations but also with the EC and ECE (Economic Commission for Europe) guidelines, so that it can be exported without any restrictions. In this case, certain parts of the vehicle must be tested by test centers that specialize in that particular field and are internationally recognized. For example, the Light-Technical Institute of the Technical University of Karlsruhe is the recognized authority in matters of lighting, the TUV in the Rhineland performs a similar function where the interior fittings and seat-belt anchorages are concerned, the Materials Testing Institute in Stuttgart looks after the belts themselves, the Materials Testing Authority in Dortmund is responsible for safety glass, and the VDE in Offenbach specializes in radio interference suppression.

When all parts subject to testing have been given a clean bill of health, the results of the tests are sent to the KBA in Flensburg, which then issues a General License to Operate. Then the vehicle manufacturer is entitled, indeed obliged, to issue a log book with each car of that model produced. The manufacturer's signature on this document signifies acceptance of responsibility that the car in question complies in all its parts with the ABE at the time of delivery to the dealer or customer.

Type approval

It does, of course, happen from time to time that a fanatical DIY fan builds a car from a variety of different makes and models, or that someone carries out a total conversion of a standard production model, for example, by converting a limousine into a convertible or installing a Porsche engine in a VW, which entails modifying the wheel suspension, springs, and brakes. The vehicle would then require a Type Approval for a Single Vehicle. An enormous amount of effort is involved, and the price is correspondingly high. Testing takes about a week, with any strength testing necessary being carried out by a technical univeristy, which would charge 15,000 to 20,000 marks for its services. On top of this, the TUV's fees would be about 10,000 marks, of which some 3,000 marks would go to cover the costs of exhaust and emission tests.

In addition to the ABE issued for complete vehicles, there are also Type Approvals issued for those parts that form a unit in themselves. Approval of this sort is required, for instance, for the wheels and steering system, exhaust units, cruise controls (tempomats, tempostats), and drive disconnection systems. The relevant TUV will issue the necessary expert opinion, at a cost of several thousand marks, and on the basis of this, the KBA in Flensburg will issue the General License to Operate. However, such an ABE may be subject to an endorsement, obliging the recipient to have the installation checked and confirmed in the vehicle log. This is the case, for instance, with spoilers, which have to be checked after attaching to ensure that the brakes receive enough cooling air and that an inadmissible level of lift is not created.

Other parts require a General Type Approval (ABG)—for example, safety glass, headlamps of all kinds, fog lamps, tail and brake lights, safety belts, tow bars, trip recorders, and many things more besides. Here again, the necessary License to Operate will be issued by the KBA in Flensburg. Every part produced after that is stamped with a letter and a code number.

Design assessment

Getting a General License to Operate is an expensive affair. A Design Assessment is a somewhat cheaper way of going about it. In such cases, a TUV center that specializes in the particular part in question inspects a sample unit and issues an assessment. The vendor must then issue a copy of this Design Assessment with every unit sold. The owner of the vehicle need only get the local TUV to confirm that the part is properly installed or attached, rather than having to have the part itself validated. An example of this would be the fitting of a different steering wheel or extended fenders.

The Design Assessment is issued in accordance with the Vehicle Registration Regulations and not in accordance with the EC and ECE guidelines.

It may sound ridiculous to have to make a visit to the local TUV because, for example, a car owner has fitted a windshield with a tinted top. However, one should not take the significance of the ABE paragraphs of the Vehicle Registration Regulations (paragraphs 19–22A) too lightly. If any modification is made to any part that is subject to a License to Operate, and if this modification is not specifically sanctioned by the TUV, then, from that moment onward, the vehicle is no longer considered to be either registered or insured, with all that this implies. Even a change of steering wheel or the use of a different size of tire not expressly approved for the vehicle concerned could lead to such a situation; and if the chassis has been lowered, well, watch out! If no License to Operate has been issued, to use the vehicle would invite an immediate summons and would mean an endorsement of the owner's license.

Not all drivers are aware that a part supplied with a Design Assessment must always be entered into the vehicle papers after inspection and approval by the local TUV; otherwise the ABE becomes invalid and the vehicle is regarded as being uninsured.

This is not the case with parts that have an ABE, with the following important exception: If the part is installed or attached, then the General License to Operate remains valid, provided that installation has been properly carried out.

Furthermore, the installation may not form part of the modification that is subject to TUV inspection and entry in the vehicle papers. Finally, the police are entitled to ask for the ABE assessment when making checks unless the conversion has been sanctioned and entered as such in the log.

Even experts can all too easily find themselves at odds with the Vehicle Registration Regulations. Where vehicle parts with a General License to Operate are concerned—for example, spoilers, rims, steering wheels, or exhaust units—special attention must be paid to two things: After certain parts have been attached or installed, a visit to the TUV and the registration authorities to have the part entered in the vehicle log is mandatory. Whether an inspection in accordance with paragraph 19 of the Vehicle Registration Regulations and subsequent entry in the vehicle log is necessary can be seen from the ABE.

An example will serve to clarify the point: Let us assume that a front spoiler that has its own ABE is attached, that this calls for changes to the airflow, and that, in addition, the car is fitted with

TÜV STUTTGART E.V.
Techn. Prüfstelle für den
Kraftfahrzeugverkehr
Typprüfstelle

Antrag- Motor-Technik-Sport GmbH   Gutachten-Nr.
steller: Mercedesstr. 1   18 10 02 0409
          7056 Weinstadt-Endersbach   Blatt 1

P r ü f b e r i c h t
über Frontspoiler

des Herstellers: Motor-Technik-Sport GmbH (MTS)
                 7056 Weinstadt-Endersbach

für: Daimler-Benz Personenkraftwagen

Typ: 123   123 D   123 C   123 T

ABE-Nr.: 9850 u. 9851 u. A309 u. A753 u.
          9850/1   9851/1   A309/1   A753/1

Ausführung: Einteiliges Formteil aus glasfaserverstärktem Kunststoff
               als Frontspoiler und Stoßstange

Anbringung: Nach Abnahme der Serienstoßstange wird der Frontspoiler mit
               4 Schrauben an dem Abschlußblech unter den Scheinwerfern und
               links und rechts je mit 2 Blechschrauben an den Radausschnit-
               ten dauerhaft befestigt.

Kenn-
zeichnung: In der Spoilermitte mit MTS und Teile-Nr. 123-01 gekenn-
               zeichnet.

Prüfergeb-
nisse: Der beschriebene Frontspoiler erfüllt die Vorschrift des
               § 32 (3) StVZO, sowie die Richtlinien über die Beschaffen-
               heit und Anbringung der äußeren Fahrzeugteile. Die Boden-
               freiheit ist durch den Anbau nicht verringert. Die Zugäng-
               lichkeit der serienmäßigen Abschleppeinrichtung ist auch
               nach Anbau des Frontspoilers gewährleistet.
               Bei Vergleichsmessungen mit dem Serienzustand konnte keine
               Verschlechterung der Bremsenkühlung durch die Anbringung des
               Frontspoilers bemerkt werden. Subjektiv konnte keine Ver-
               änderung des Fahr-, Lenk- und Bremsverhaltens festgestellt
               werden. Die Höchstgeschwindigkeit bleibt im Rahmen der Meß-
               genauigkeit unverändert.

Gegen den Anbau und die Begutachtung gem. § 19 (2) StVZO des Frontspoilers
an den oben angeführten Daimler-Benz Personenkraftwagen bestehen keine
technischen Bedenken.

Anlage
Fotos Frontspoiler   2 6. FEB. 1982
                                          Der amtlich anerkannte Sachverständige
Stuttgart, den   Dipl.-Ing.
TYP-Gü/Ah

                                          (Günter)

Dieses Gutachten ist nur gültig, wenn es mit einem grauen Balken überdruckt ist.

Front spoiler with air channeling for engine and brakes. TÜV assessment of a front spoiler.

wider wheels and tires. In this case, a visit to the TÜV is necessary in order to obtain official confirmation that the vehicle is safe to be on the road and, thus, to ensure that the ABE and the insurance remain valid.

There are two things that interest the authorities:

- If the cooling air guides are not correctly attached, or not attached at all, it is possibly a case of incorrect assembly. The brakes could overheat, and the vehicle is not safe to be on the road.
- As a rule, wheels and tires wider than those offered by the manufacturer have no ABE and need to be entered in the vehicle papers. Not infrequently, the addition of such wheels is subject to special conditions, such as adequate

bodywork covering of the running surface of the tires, for example, by a front spoiler. In this case, the front spoiler, as an indirect form of wheel covering, would require approval. It is therefore advisable to read the ABE documents extremely carefully in order to fulfill all the conditions laid down concerning approval so as to avoid any programs at all in case of police checks or an accident.

Of the bodywork accessory parts available, the front spoiler can have the greatest effect on the driving characteristics and the safety of a car. In the true sense of the phrase, it is "up front" and can therefore have a decisive influence on drag and the road adhesion of the tires.

Three factors are predominantly in the mind of the designer of front spoilers: brake cooling, downpressure, drag.

TUV tests

The first and most important of the tests carried out by the TUV is the braking test. As part of this test, comparative trials are carried out against an unmodified production car of the same type and model to measure the changes. The so-called cooling curve, for example, is determined in this way. This means the extent to which the heat produced by the braking pads is taken away by the airflow produced during travel. The brake pads are heated up to a prescribed temperature, for example, 300°C, by braking. The temperature is measured directly at the pads by a temperature sensing device. This device later shows how the brakes cool down of their own accord at a constant speed of 130 km/h due to the effect of the airflow. Such parameters for approval are laid down in guidelines and precisely defined. In order to obtain the TUV's blessing, the degree of brake cooling achieved must be at least as good as that of the production car.

A considerable proportion of today's production cars have brakes that have been optimized to reduce both their cost and their weight. This can lead to major problems during inspection if the airflow over the brakes is changed as a result of the addition of a front spoiler. The situation can be particularly critical if the front spoiler is very deep, requiring additional channeling of air to the brakes.

Another important aspect of the approval of a front spoiler by the TUV is the measurement of the downpressure or lift on the front and rear axles. The lift and downpressure are those additional forces that act on the wheel in question while the car is in motion to hold it on the road. In the case of lift, the downward forces decrease as the speed increases, that is, the car becomes lighter and road-holding decreases. This often happens, although the lifting force in modern cars is mostly relatively low.

If a passenger car weighs, for example, 1000 kg, with the weight distributed evenly over all four wheels, then 250 kg acts on each of the wheels. At a speed of 200 km/h, the upward force acting on the front axle would be equivalent to 40 kg. This would result in each wheel being loaded with 230 kg, or ninety-two percent loading.

It is therefore extremely important to ensure that the lift and downpressure values of the production car are not jeopardized when adding bodywork accessories, such as front and rear spoilers and wings. With front spoilers in particular, it is important to ensure that there are sufficient surfaces designed to produce downpressure.

Most serially produced cars have relatively harmless front spoilers. Even those that are not specifically designed for the purpose are mainly adequate to fulfill the criteria regarding downpressure. In most cases, all that is required is a good "shovel," and the necessary downpressure is achieved.

There are points that can impose limitations, and the TUV checks these as well:

- The distance between the bottom edge of the spoiler and the ground may not be less than a certain minimum figure in order not to impose too great a restriction on the general suitability of the car for use on the road. For example, if the vehicle went down on its suspension on an uneven road, the spoiler could catch on a manhole cover.
- The bodywork accessories added on may not project significantly beyond the limits of the vehicle in its production form, that is, beyond bumpers, wings, and the like. If this does occur, then the new dimensions must be entered in the vehicle log. The expert must check carefully that the overhanging parts satisfy the safety requirements, ensuring that no sharp edges or other parts that could cause injury are left exposed.
- The front spoiler also influences the downpressure on the rear axle. If an excessively high downpressure is created at the front end, this can cause increasing lift at the rear. In many cases, it is therefore mandatory to enter details of a front spoiler that has a corresponding rear spoiler. It is forbidden to use the front spoiler on its own in such cases.

In addition, it is important to remember, as with the rear apron, that it may be necessary on occasion to tow a car away.

It is immaterial to the legislator—so far as current regulations are concerned at least—whether the coefficient of drag (C_d) or the wind resistance ($C_d \times A$) change after the addition of any accessory parts, so long as they remain within the permissible limits of deviation for approval of the vehicle in general. A minimal deviation is permissible at top speed; however, if this increases by any measurable amount, say by 8 km/h, then the deviation can easily be measured and will call for corresponding changes in the vehicle log.

The same applies to any changes in engine performance or fuel consumption. If the changes remain within the limits set by the manufacturer or within the legal tolerances, there is no cause for concern. Major changes, however, are subject to approval and require entry in the vehicle papers. Such changes frequently occur if different tire sizes are used.

On the whole, however, there is still enough room to maneuver for those who wish to add a front spoiler on their own responsibility, since the TUV does not relieve them of all responsibility in such matters.

Rocker panels and rear aprons, on the other hand, are simpler to handle from a technical point of view. In the case of rocker panels, it is basically necessary only to ensure that the jacking points of the production model are retained or that suitable special jacks are provided with the car.

For the rest, rocker panels are largely a matter of taste. Their aerodynamic importance, compared with front spoilers, is relatively modest, although theoretical calculations and a number of wind tunnel experiments suggest that the air stream between the wheels is calmed by smooth-surfaced aprons and the C_d value correspondingly improved.

Practically all rocker panels have one advantage, which comes at the cost of a minor drawback. The dirt that accumulates on the sides of a car, and that in modern cars can reach almost up to the midline, is considerably reduced, but this in turn means that, in stepping into the car, one must pick up one's feet somewhat higher than usual to avoid getting mud on pant legs.

On the other hand, the rocker panel is a decisive factor where styling is concerned—the preferred outline after conversion is very definitely wide and low.

It is reasonable to expect that, in future, a considerable amount of effort will be invested in fitting rocker panels to top-quality cars. Rocker panels that could be lowered for high speeds would create a suction effect underneath the car that would improve the road-holding.

This in turn would make it possible to design the remaining parts of the bodywork specifically to reduce drag and to assign priority to down-

Rear apron and rocker panels are easier to handle from a technical point of view. With rocker panels, it is merely necessary to retain the jacking point. Wide tires must always be entered in the log. Extended fenders enclose the wide wheels.

pressure only at times when it is absolutely necessary, that is, at high or very high speed.

At low speeds, front spoilers, rear aprons, and rocker panels, which might be lowered, would not significantly affect the suitability of the car for everyday motoring—for example, if the car was driven up over a curb—compared to a car of the same type that did not have these additional features. When the car was driven at high speed, however, the aerodynamic shape and the additional low pressure created under the floor of the car in the relatively tightly sealed area bounded by the accessory parts would have a doubly positive effect on the road-holding.

Bearing in mind that improvements in the C_d value of the next generation of cars will only be achieved at increasingly heavy cost in terms of investment, since the results achieved are already very good, one can see that such relatively expensive developments, designed to produce a suction effect on the underside of the car body, and their impact on the C_d value and the downpressure will be of the greatest importance.

The best ground effect would be achieved with a funnel-shaped, smooth car floor closed off at the sides, such as is currently used on racing cars. However, this involves expensive secondary measures, such as spoilers and rocker panels that can be lowered; sophisticated engine, transmission, and exhaust system cooling due to the fully paneled car floor; and aerodynamic optimization of the wheel suspension and braking mechanism—possibly also paneled and with special channeling of cooling air.

The aerodynamic effect of a rear apron is even less certain than that of the rocker panels. One can accordingly assume that the rear spoiler mainly used in conjunction with it plays a significantly greater part in the effect produced. The rear apron is usually more of a stylistic termination to the line of the sides of the car, which starts with the front spoiler and the rocker panels and carries through to the rear. It is for this reason above all that rocker panels are attached only behind the wheels.

The advantage of most rear aprons is mainly to be found in the visual enhancement they provide, since they make the rear of the car look more solid and in many cases also cover up the underside of the spare wheel well, which is clearly visible and forms an ugly bulge on many production cars, as well as the exhaust system, which is scarcely a thing of beauty either. However, it is absolutely essential to ensure—and this applies not only to designers, but also to the TUV experts and the customers—that the rear apron is never attached too close to the exhaust pipe. Often no exhaust baffles are provided to extend the end section of the pipe, so that exhaust gases can build up under the rear apron, creating all manner of trouble.

Not only can this result in exhaust gases finding their way into the car through the floor, but the whole issue can become a very hot one, indeed a burning one. The rear apron could catch fire or at least smolder—often enough fanned by the wind. Admittedly, there is a provision in the TUV approval procedure concerning the fire resistance of the materials used, but it isn't possible to require that they be completely incombustible.

Extended fenders serve a useful purpose only if they are used to enclose wide wheels and tires. Otherwise, they merely create drag (the C_d value is reduced) and they also increase the cross-sectional area of the car.

Where extended fenders are used, it is essential to ensure that they are securely anchored and do not tear, sticking out like spears and presenting a hazard to other road users.

Other styling by-products, such as wind splits and special trim, are of no technical importance. They originated for the most part in racing, where they perform a useful and necessary function and are generally of larger dimensions.

Much the same applies to the majority of radiator grilles. They often merely serve to make the car more distinctive than the corresponding production model. Here again it is frequently possible, with a bit of effort, to make a technical contribution to the car's suitability for everyday motoring: On the one hand, by doing away with fragmented frontal areas, one can improve the drag value; on the other hand, the lighting can also be improved by providing more or better headlamps, in many types of car at least. However, proper cooling must be assured as before by installing a flat-surfaced "nose."

Apart from front spoilers, rear airflow guides in the form of rear spoilers or wings have the greatest effect on the aerodynamics of the car. As with front spoilers, both the coefficient of drag (C_d) and the downpressure are decisively affected. In addition, due to its exposed position, the rear spoiler or wing is subject to careful testing to ensure that it does not constitute a danger to other road users in case of an accident.

While it is very difficult to make any general statements concerning the effect of rear spoilers and wings on the C_d value, it is in all cases true to say that downpressure is increased proportionally the larger the surface area of the rear spoiler and the greater the angle at which it is set. The latter is in practice only possible to a limited extent, as the wing would otherwise act more like a braking parachute. As a rule, a rear spoiler generates considerable downpressure on the rear axle. This is why the simultaneous mounting of a front spoiler is often recommended, or even mandatory, in order to compensate for the resultant lightening of the front axle loading.

Until quite recently, one could assume that only rear spoilers of soft rubber would meet with the approval of the TUV. This has now changed, and rear spoilers and wings are now available not only in hard materials such as sheet metal or GRP, with a wide rubber strip to give protection against impact, but also of GRP alone. This is possible because the legally permitted limiting values for the maximum deceleration of a test body—simulating collision with a pedestrian in an accident—can be improved on by designing a suitable spoiler or wing made of GRP.

In any case, very special attention must be paid to the shape of such parts, since rear spoilers and wings must on no account project or have any sharp edges. For this reason, great attention is paid during inspection and approval to the distance between the bodywork and the spoiler or wing, as well as the outside radii of the wing and the point of transition to the bodywork. The means by which the spoiler or wing is attached is also closely examined, since these parts are sometimes subjected to very high stresses at high speed, due to the force exerted by the wind.

The breakaway edges increasingly available over the last few years, which are applied to the lid of the car trunk, occupy a rather uncertain position. On the one hand, they cannot be quite so sharp-edged as the rubber spoilers are, relatively speaking, but on the other hand they do offer some slight aerodynamic advantages over the smooth-surfaced trunk lid since, if they are correctly shaped, they appear to lead to more efficient breakaway of the air stream.

Rear airflow guides in the form of rear spoilers or wings affect the aerodynamics by changing the coefficient of drag and the downpressure. They are also carefully checked to ensure that they cannot result in injuries in the event of an accident.

Chapter 3

From concept to concrete

The first problem to be solved when manufacturing molds and parts is to decide on the most suitable material. Depending on the production volumes, the bodywork part, and the purpose for which it is intended, the specific characteristics of a given material may possibly have a negative effect on the performance of the car in later use.

The following criteria play a decisive role: energy absorption on impact, material behavior with changing temperature, willingness of the surface to accept paint.

As already mentioned, there are different methods of manufacturing bodywork parts. In essence, three types of material are used: metal—sheet steel or aluminum, hard plastics, soft plastics.

Sheet steel or aluminum is rarely used today since these materials require either very high tooling costs for presses or fabrication by hand. In addition, given the relatively small numbers of parts involved and the fact that they have to be riveted or welded onto the bodywork, the use of metal is simply not justifiable. Assembly of such parts calls for a very high level of manual skill, especially from the bodywork builder.

Furthermore, the fitting is extremely labor-intensive, and only a small number of specialists can be used, at correspondingly high rates of pay. Such expenditure is restricted to very expensive conversion projects. The cost of the remaining spoiler accessories already runs into five figures.

Extended fenders and spoiler edges mounted on the trunk lid are to some extent an exception since the parts have relatively small surface areas and are flat; they can be riveted in position, the gaps filled in, and the whole area sprayed over, even when plastic parts are used.

In general, the choice of material comes down to plastics of one type or another. Here again, there are basically three types: glass-fiber-reinforced plastics (GRP), deep-drawn foil, foam materials.

GRP's are resins interlayered with glass fiber in the form of mats, fabrics, or short fibers, which solidify when accelerators are added and can be used to produce hard, very strong parts that can be relatively highly stressed. The basic substance—the body—is provided by the resin, while the strength and elasticity are derived from the glass fibers.

The advantage of working with GRP is that the negatives, that is, the casts of the models that correspond to the parts to be produced at a later stage, are likewise of glass fiber and therefore represent only a relatively small proportion of the development costs. This is true of so-called hand-laminated parts, that is, accessory parts produced individually by hand. In this way, the investment in tooling can be justified, even with small production volumes.

Deep-drawing with plastic slabs, that is, foil deep-drawing, is considerably more expensive, but still acceptable with relatively small batch sizes.

Parts made in this way are approximately 1.5 to 2.0 mm thick and extremely close-fitting if proper care is taken in preparing the prototypes. However, they have the disadvantage that the

This interesting styling drawing comes from the Daimler-Benz studio. On a W124 chassis, it's dated July 3, 1980.

Full-size and obviously realistic designs are created with special clay over wooden mockup constructions. From these full-size, finished designs molds and press tools can be created.

40

hard material is relatively brittle and breaks very easily, especially at sub-zero temperatures. Cracks can develop as a result of the residual stresses left over from assembly and further exacerbated by driving, even without any external impact. The principal parts made from deep-drawn foil are radiator grilles, front spoilers, rocker panels, and rear aprons.

In the early days of visual styling, foam materials suffered from the enormous drawbacks of being highly porous and absorbing a lot of moisture. The first time they were subjected to frost, the result was predictable—and the damage plain for all to see.

Now, however, foam materials are among the best production materials available from the point of view of quality. Particularly high strength combined with surprising elasticity are the hallmarks of foams interlayered with glass fibers. The tooling costs involved in producing parts made of such materials are, however, enormously high and can only be recouped on the sort of production runs no small or medium-size styling company could hope to aspire to.

For economic reasons, then, there are limits to what can be achieved with foam. If any changes are made to production models, or if the market has not been accurately assessed, it is impossible to respond as quickly or as easily as with GRP parts. By the very nature of the materials used, foam parts are liable to change shape on aging or under the effect of heat, while the inner tensions in the material, induced for example by their mountings, are gradually reduced. After a certain period of time, such parts no longer fit precisely and become badly warped.

In order to take a more realistic look at a new shape or concept, models of the new car are made in wood and clay. After spraying, these "cars" are subjected to detailed testing, and the final choice of model to be developed is then made.

Chapter 4

"Let the buyer beware"

The DIY approach to fitting bodywork accessories calls for a certain amount of caution. Only if detailed and clearly understandable assembly instructions are available is the work likely to be successful. Of course, it requires not only a certain amount of technical understanding but also a considerable measure of manual skill to attach, for example, a front spoiler or a rear apron, especially since every production car has its own tolerances, which must be scrupulously observed when attaching add-on parts. The part should sit firmly in position and be totally free from stress, even after the paint has been applied. The special tools required for the job, such as drilling tools, collet chuck, lacquering set and so on, must also be available.

A buyer of bodywork parts should remember that one day, sooner or later, the vehicle may be up for sale. Quite apart from the more extreme forms of conversion or enhancement, which are likely to attract few buyers in the used car market, as little damage as possible should be done to the car when attaching the parts. For example, any holes, slots, or incisions made can provide an opportunity for rust to creep in if they are not sealed off at once with the greatest care—which, unfortunately, is all too often overlooked.

The ideal way to attach such goodies is to use the bore holes, screws, and clips already present. Of course, it would be even better if the new parts were direct replacements for existing parts of the production car and could be attached in exactly the same manner and place. If

it is necessary to modify the bodywork to take the new parts, only the absolute minimum number of holes should be made.

Parts that create cavities between themselves and the bodywork are particularly prone to the formation of rust if moisture is allowed to seep in, and especially if there are large areas of metal without a protective coating of paint. This is often the case, for example, with extended fenders.

It would, of course, be far better if the parts were attached in such a way that they could easily be removed again when the vehicle is offered for sale. Styling fans should give some thought to possible trade-in values before they start drilling holes in the top of the wings, the engine hood, and the trunk, or even the roof. Such measures call for a considerable degree of enthusiasm for styling anyway.

Anyone considering styling modifications should always check first to see whether the add-on parts involved already have an approval certificate, or whether they need to be entered into the vehicle papers. This advice should on no account be taken lightly, because if such parts need to be entered in the vehicle registration papers, the log book, and above all, the vehicle registration certificate, and they are not, the owner or driver could be in for some very unpleasant surprises in case of an accident, up to and including the loss of insurance coverage.

Smoked or darkened rear lights provide an apparently harmless example of this. If these do not have TUV approval and another car runs into

42

the back of the car fitted with them, it could well happen that the owner of the modified car would have to bear at least a part of the costs, because the lighting would be deemed to be inadequate.

The situation could become particularly critical if the parts attached constitute a danger to other road users, for example, rear wings with sharp edges. In such cases, it is entirely conceivable that if another person sustained injuries in this way as a result of an accident, the owner could face a charge of causing actual bodily harm. And that is no joke—quite apart from the fact that in such cases, any insurance company would withdraw insurance coverage on the grounds of gross negligence. The same would also apply in the case of wide wheels that had not been approved, which could possibly result in failure of the wheel suspension or other vital components.

So there are limits to what one can do in the way of styling and modifications, a point where the fun ends and the risks begin—both for the owner and for other road users. However, if all the regulations regarding approval are scrupulously observed, then pride of ownership is not diluted with sorrow and regrets.

Chapter 5

Chassis modifications

In no area of automobile technology is the gap between the demands and the necessary compromises reached so vast as in the conception of cars with top speeds of over 200 km/h; with top-class models, these speeds can even exceed 300 km/h.

A jumbo jet, for example, comes in to land at a speed of just over 200 km/h. Driving a car at the same or higher speeds could therefore be compared to low-level flying. Admittedly, the pilot trims the aircraft constantly, so as to achieve the optimum speed for landing: Landing flaps and slats are extended, the flipper trimmed, and the undercarriage lowered.

When a car is driven at top speeds of more than 200 km/h, continual adjustments are scarcely possible. Nevertheless, they really ought to be, since aerodynamics play an important role at such speeds. The increase in wind resistance is of the order of the third power of the speed—in other words, wind resistance at 200 km/h is not twice as high as at 100 mh/h, but eight times, and at 300 km/h not three times, but twenty-seven. In addition, the lift to which the car is subject at the time must be kept within limits. This is achieved, of course, by adding spoilers. In contrast to airplanes, however, cars are not adjustable, with certain exceptions. They can only provide optimum results at a given speed.

Modern high-performance cars are expected to show flexible characteristics in all conditions, irrespective of whether they are backing or cornering, or whether they are lightly or heavily laden. Thus the modern car chassis has

nothing more to do with the rough and ready machinery of yesteryear. Massive axles and thick packets of leaf springs can still be found, but are really only necessary in extremely heavy commercial vehicles. A handy and comfortable passenger car requires filigreelike work, with precision mechanics and sophisticated balancing and tuning.

But the parts that contribute to good driving behavior should not take up too much space here either. The four wheels of a car enclose only a very small part of the world. To convert as much as possible of this into a useful space—this is an important aspect of chassis construction.

The more powerful the engine and the greater the performance of a car, the more severe are the demands made on the individual chassis components. The tires eliminate the majority of jolts coming up from the road surface. More substantial bumps are absorbed by the suspension and damping; rubber bearings between the bodywork and the chassis eliminate vibrations; and even the seats play their part, being carefully designed to provide selective absorption.

Acceleration, braking, and steering exert considerable forces in various directions, to which the chassis must be equal. These stresses are taken care of by means of carefully computed suspension geometry, which is sensitive to every movement. The "track-stabilizing steering roller radius," for example, prevents the car's departing from its proper line as a result of the effects of unevenness in the road surface on the

The wheel has long been considered as one of man's principal inventions, but it has changed over the course of the centuries. The principle, however, has remained the same—a rolling disk with a shaft through the middle. (1) a solid wooden wheel from the Viking era (ca. 900); (2) wooden-spoked wheel on a ceremon- ial coach made for King Ludwig II (ca. 1885); (3) wire- spoked wheel on the Daimler steel-wheeled car (1888–89); (4) wooden-spoked wheel on Amadee Bol- lee's car (1900); (5) wheel with pressed steel rim; (6) wheel with light-alloy cast rim.

front wheels when the car brakes. Invisible helpers distribute the braking force over the front and rear wheels, with the principal work being carried out by the front disk brakes.

The problems that stand in the way of such an objective are quite clear. A soft and well-balanced chassis guarantees a comfortable journey on the one hand, due to its ability to neutralize even the major effects of unevenness in the road surface. On the other hand, it reduces the pleasure of sports car driving because the tangible feeling of contact with the car's behavior and the responses of the suspension is restricted. A taut, even hard suspension, on the other hand, enables the car to be driven in a sporting fashion, with a high degree of safety right up to the limit, but often proves to be very uncomfortable and tiring over long distances or in urban driving, and often so tiring that the driver becomes quite aggressive.

Stiff international competition led to rapid technical development and to a positive explosion of new ideas and techniques in the field of engine design. Almost inevitably, developments in the bodywork followed, with individual wishes fulfilled by the chassis specialists. Yet all these

measures—whether for normal everyday motoring or for sporting purposes—boil down to safety at higher speeds:
- higher limiting speeds when cornering
- better control at the top end of the speed range
- good directional stability
- low susceptibility to crosswinds
- optimum power transmission
- more effective brakes

Optimizing the chassis of a car is not a matter for the layman or amateur and should be left to those clearly qualified for the task. These specialists offer kits specially adapted to a particular type of vehicle, which are then given written approval by the TUV.

The sort of specific measures carried out on the chassis include changing the behavior of the suspension and damping, lowering the chassis, widening the track.

This can involve changing shock absorbers, springs, stabilizer bars, rims, and tires.

Installation of firmer shock absorbers is one of the most common steps taken to improve a chassis, as it is relatively simple to perform. The so-called racing shock absorbers are types that are capable of meeting higher performance

standards in function and service life than the absorbers used in everyday motoring. Naturally, one must take into account that the greater the damping factor, the more comfort is impaired.

Fundamental research in this field is undertaken by the automobile industry, while practical experience is gained in racing. Damping is a form of compromise between good road-holding and pleasant ride comfort. Damping characteristics are designed to be rather more taut in cars designed to be driven in a sporting fashion, in order to optimize road-holding even in extreme driving conditions. Special absorbers—for example, those produced by Koni—permit differential adjustment. Complete kits of parts, including specially matched springs and already approved by TUV, are available for ambitious drivers. In this way, the vehicle can also be lowered.

For some time now, electronics have been an integral part of chassis design. Various series manufacturers sing the praises of the electronic chassis. With this type of chassis, the hardness of the damping and the ground clearance are automatically adjusted to the state of the road surface, the driving situation, the vehicle load, and the speed—all in a flash and with the utmost reliability.

In order to achieve this, sensors constantly measure acceleration and deceleration, angle of roll, amount of turn on the steering, the height of the vehicle front and rear, the vehicle speed, and the engine load. The measurement data are processed by a microprocessor, which issues the appropriate commands for the chassis adjustments. Regulation takes place, for example, by means of air suspension elements via the four transverse control arms. The suspension and damping are made softer or tauter and the ground clearance increased or decreased by either supplying or removing air, just enough to meet the requirement of the moment.

Other firms offer damping that can be adjusted by hand—the system with three-fold electronically adjustable gas-pressure shock absorbers, which the driver can adjust by means of a switch. In this process, a motor built into each of the four shock absorbers is actuated by a central control unit, and this regulates the rate of

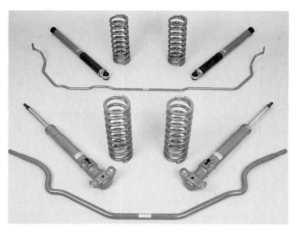

Suspension kit for sports cars from Carlsson: gas-filled control arm inserts, gas-filled shock absorbers with sports springs, stabilizer bars—for lowering suspension by 40 mm.

Front shock absorber unit on Mercedes 190 E 2.3-16 (W 201).

flow of the hydraulic oil by a valve, thereby regulating the hardness of the absorber. The driver can thus choose between three levels of damping—soft, medium, and hard.

Anyone who uses a car for competition purposes gives more than a passing thought to the transverse stabilizer bars. The standard ver-

sions installed in production cars are often of limited efficiency when the car is driven in a sporting fashion. If they are strengthened and suitably adapted to the type of vehicle in question, the roll when cornering can be noticeably reduced and the safety and stability decisively improved.

As this involves a fairly complex level of modification that cannot be carried out by simply any firm, one would be well advised to seek advice from an expert before undertaking such a modification and to go for a trial run in a car that has already had the modification carried out.

The same applies to lowering the overall height of the car, which is achieved by installing shorter springs. This has the effect of lowering the mass center of gravity, which in turn has a positive effect on ride stability and safety, provided that suitable shock absorbers are also installed. However, this results in shorter spring travel, and thus a reduction in ride comfort. The firm carrying out the modification should advise on the extent to which the permissible loading would be reduced as a result.

However, there are limits to the extent that a car can be lowered if it is to remain usable for everyday motoring. In general, this will vary with the type of car and the springs retained from the production model. The chassis should be lowered by about 3.0 to 3.5 cm at the most, since other-

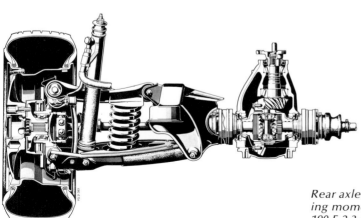

Rear axle shock absorber unit with starting and braking moment support and level control on Mercedes 190 E 2.3-16 (W 201).

47

wise the balance between the springs, the damping, the wheel suspension, and the wheels themselves could suffer considerably, and could even finish up worse than in the original "long-legged" and unmodified form. There is also the matter of reduced ground clearance and, if the lowering has been excessive, the negative effects on the loading of the suspension elements. Furthermore, any expert would advise against replacing only the springs and not the shock absorbers as well. This is admittedly a matter of the individual purse, but the shock absorbers and springs do form a unit. In this context, it is not only the individual tuning firms that will give this advice, but also the manufacturer of the special components, such as Bilstein, Boge, Fichtel & Sachs, or Koni. There have already been cases in which serious accidents have occurred as a result of springs dropping out because the wheel still had the original shock absorbers.

Other modifications to be made to the chassis concern the track—the wider this is, the more closely the car will hug the road. In earlier days, spacer rings or disks were installed on the wheel hubs. Nowdays, this broadening effect is achieved mostly by wheels with a different degree of wheel offset. However, one should not forget to check whether extended fenders are necessary, if possible in conjunction with wider wheels and tires, and whether the greater track width could lead to excessive stressing of the suspension and shock absorber mountings on the bodywork, to increased wear on joints, drive shafts, and bearings, and to considerably impaired straight-line characteristics.

The object of fitting wider wheels and tires is to take advantage of the extra tire adhesion surface and the greater lateral support forces provided by the lower tire wall, resulting in improved straight-line and cornering stability. Here again, certain sacrifices must be accepted where the inherent resilience of the tires is concerned, affecting the suspension and ride comfort.

Nowadays such enhancements would be almost unthinkable without the enormous variety of light-alloy wheels—lighter, wider, and lovelier, they say—that help to reduce the weight of the unsprung mass of the car. As a result, the effect of a bad road surface transmitted through the wheels to the bodywork is reduced. Comfort is increased and road-holding is improved. Another good characteristic of light-alloy wheels, their truer running, is almost tangible to a sensitive driver. As a casting, every light-alloy wheel must be accurately finished, so that any out-of-roundness is virtually ruled out from the start. With normal steel wheels, on the other hand, certain tolerances in height and axial runout, always within limits, of course, must be accepted from the start.

But when buying light-alloy wheels, one must consider individual taste—aesthetic feelings combined with the desire to express one's own individuality. Men in particular are very keen on these special accessories, which undoubtedly enhance the appearance of the car in their eyes and underline their own individuality, reflecting something of the image of the Grand Prix racing driver on the front row of the grid.

Does anything go, then, so far as wider wheels and tires are concerned? The question is not all that easy, although wide wheels are becoming increasingly available from the factory and form part of every stylist's stock in trade. Many of the special wheels available in the trade have an ABE or a type sample certificate. If they have an ABE, the new wide wheels can be fitted without having to take the car to the TUV for approval—assuming that the wheel and tire sizes are already entered in the Vehicle Registration Certificate. If only the wheel or the tire—or perhaps neither—has been approved by the manufacturer in the vehicle papers, the owner must take the car to the TUV when the new wheels and tires are fitted. There are certain types of tires that may be used only in conjunction with certain wheel sizes, and many of them have certain conditions attached to them concerning bodywork modifications, such as wheel housings.

Naturally, it would be wrong to think that extremely wide tires alone will get you to paradise. There must be a sensible relationship between the tires and the size of vehicle and the engine performance. It would be entirely misplaced to think in terms of the size of tires used by Formula 1 racing cars.

With racing cars, the frictional connection between tires and track is artificially improved by means of toothlike or adhesive effects. The combinations of racing tires give rise, at suitable temperatures, to a softening process comparable to the effect of an all-purpose glue.

However, such tires are not suitable for normal motoring. They would be much too sensitive. In spite of that, the tires used for high-speed motoring have to satisfy stringent additional standards of safety and comfort.

One thing is absolutely certain: The trend toward wide tires continues unabated because the light-alloy wheels are, for the most part, undoubtedly more attractive.

The range of tire sizes and cross sections available on the market does not make it any easier to select the right one. If a tire manufacturer really wants to sell products to the styling firms, it needs to have some 300 types, differing in size, shape, and speed, available.

Even in this area, the automobile industry is competing with the styling companies. Wider tires are now available on request from the factory for any class of car and any performance range. The series manufacturers are having at least certain types of wide tire approved by the KBA for later conversions of production cars.

Anyone wishing to graduate from wide to super-wide tires should be quite clear about the potential consequences before taking such a step. Excessively high steering forces are compensated for by servo assistance, at least in cars at the top end of the middle range and upward, but unresponsive straight-line driving characteristics and excessive reaction to ruts in the road surface can be rather disturbing. But drivers with sporting ambitions are rarely put off by these things, since the tire manufacturers make sure that even tires for high speeds are both safe and adequately comfortable.

However, a very dangerous situation could arise if tires designed for such extreme demands are worn down to the minimum tread level permitted. Hydroplaning could then occur before the famous—or infamous—80 km/h danger point is actually reached.

Naturally, greater weight has an effect on tires, too—though this is to some extent compensated for by light-alloy wheels—as well as on ride comfort and driving characteristics. Tires form part of the unsprung mass of the car. In the final analysis, the sporting characteristics of the car, evidenced by improved handling, will predominate. However, even better results would be obtained by adapting the entire chassis and using appropriate shock absorbers and springs.

Light-alloy wheel by Lorinser: lighter, wider, and more attractive.

Chapter 6

Engine tuning

The desire to have more horsepower available under the hood is perfectly understandable, since, with sensible driving, it means greater comfort and safety. In addition, the driver's enjoyment is immeasurably increased. The automobile industry caters to the customer's demand for increased horsepower by providing a wide range of engines. If the manufacturer cannot meet the requirement, the customer will turn to the tuner.

In contrast to the number of chassis specially modified for sporting purposes, "doctored" power units are installed only in very small numbers. Almost every volume producer now offers a top-range model with turbo or four-valve technology within its product range. Only in the top price bracket does one find any increase in the swept volume of engines again.

Tuning specialists, however, tailor their products to the wishes of their customers. Mercedes drivers, in particular, are an odd lot in this respect. So far as tuning is concerned, it is turbocharger technology that has taken over with a vengeance. The weaknesses of supercharged engines at low revs are in general well known.

The reverse side of the coin is generally easy to recognize in a normally tuned engine. Increases in the performance of a given power unit lead to changes in the torque and output characteristics. If the power unit is to produce more power at higher engine speeds, then the power curve in the lower speed range will frequently fall, that is, the engine loses torque in this range, as well as elasticity.

What are the possibilities, then, for improved engine performance? Greater horsepower can be obtained, for example, by increasing the amount of air inducted. There are various ways of going about it:

- Increasing the cylinder capacity. This solution involves a larger and heavier engine, and, above all, increased mechanical friction within the machine.
- Increasing engine speed. This calls for strengthening of many engine parts, due to the increased centrifugal forces. It also increases the friction losses.
- Increasing the density of the charge. The increased performance attainable through such measures (for example, polishing the intake channels, reduction of flow losses) is relatively modest.
- Supercharging the engine. This solution enables performance to be increased and maximum torque to be raised without increasing engine speeds. In most cases, the swept volume does not need to be enlarged. The engine load is increased, though.

Previously, it was often enough to fit a sports exhaust system and a multiple carburetor system. If that did not produce the required increase in performance, then larger valves and a special "hot" camshaft for longer valve operating times were added. The improved cylinder charge and resulting increase in engine output frequently led to increased consumption, and to greater wear if the engine's greater willingness to work as exploited to the full. In addition to that, the engine became increasingly less elastic the greater the cylinder capacity.

Another method of tuning is by machining the cylinder head in the vicinity of the gas ducts and combustion chambers. This "fine grinding" is designed to improve the swirling of the fresh charge and reduce the friction along the walls of the intake and outlet manifolds. As tuning becomes more widespread and the pressures of competition increase, precision modifications, at least so far as top-class tuners are concerned, become increasingly subordinate to the massive mechanical modifications undertaken, generally involving installation of a supercharger or a larger engine from one of the manufacturer's other series.

There are two possible systems to force-feed an engine with fresh air by means of a supercharger:
- compressor (mechanical supercharger)—for example, vane-type pump or rotary piston pump (Roots blower), spiral charger (G-charger on VW), Wankel supercharger (Ro super-charger)
- turbocharger

Supercharging

Even while the development of the motor car was still in its infancy, the pioneers of engine design and construction had no doubt that there were limits to filling the cylinders of a car with a mixture of gas and air. They did not want to have to rely solely on the suction effect produced by the piston, but wanted to force the fresh gases into the combustion chambers in order to achieve a better filling, and thus greater performance. Louis Renault was the first one to give serious thought, in a patent application dated 1902, to the question of "increasing the pressure of the gases in the cylinders."

Seven years later, a Swiss named Buchi hit upon the idea of exploiting the energy latent in the exhaust gases to drive a centrifugal compressor, using a turbine as well. He drew up a patent on "pulsating supercharging" of piston engines. At the same time, Marius Berliet was carrying out experiments on supercharging with the aid of a precompressor.

The problems of supercharging engines became increasingly urgent, especially as a result of the enormous progress in aviation technology before and during World War I. With airplane engines in particular, it was clear that performance fell off sharply at high altitudes due to the associated drop in pressure. Even while World War I was in progress, an Italian, Anastasi, took out a patent on the use of a supercharging system in aircraft. Also in 1917, the engineer Rateau registered a series of patents that addressed themselves to the principles of supercharging.

The first system used for supercharging car engines was the compressor. In later years, as so often happens, motor racing served as a sort of pacemaker. In 1923, a Fiat powered by forced induction was entered in a Grand Prix race. In the course of time, more and more manufacturers of sports and racing cars went over to this type of system: Alfa Romeo, Auto-Union, Bugatti, Delage, Maserati, Mercedes.

After World War II, the supercharger, and in particular the exhaust-gas-driven turbocharger, underwent enormous technical improvements and became much more reliable. Both systems were chiefly used to increase the performance of diesel engines (locomotives, trucks). As motor sport's regulations did not permit exhaust-gas-driven turbochargers to be used, these slipped further and further from the minds of racing engineers and designers.

It was only at the beginning of the 1960's that the exhaust-gas-driven turbocharger reappeared on the motoring scene. Regulations were now less stringent and biased against it. It was reborn in the United States. In 1961, the first production passenger car with an exhaust-gas-driven turbocharger was introduced, the Chevrolet Corvair. It also clearly demonstrated its superiority in the famous Indianapolis 500 at the time, in the Offenhauser engine.

At the beginning of 1970, Porsche equipped its 917 series cars with two exhaust-gas-driven turbochargers. The twelve-cylinder engine had a swept volume of 4.5, and later 5.0 liters, and produced up to 1200 hp. This car dominated the CanAm series, which was one of the most important sports car racing series at the beginning of the 1970's (it took place in Canada and the United States—hence the name). Other manufacturers followed Porsche's example and also started installing turbochargers.

Today, both Formula 1 and Indy racing cars and sports racing cars scarcely stand a chance of winning unless they have a turbocharger. Admittedly, just recently, the turbocharger has met increasing competition, both in production and in racing cars, from the mechanical supercharger. And of course no one would expect the tuners to ignore the writing on the wall.

How superchargers work

In a normally aspirated conventional gas engine, built on the four-stroke principle, more than thirty-five percent of the energy supplied to the engine in the form of fuel is lost again with exhaust gases. The flow and thermal energy in the hot exhaust gases cannot be utilized in any way.

However, a proportion of the energy otherwise lost with the exhaust gases can be recovered by means of the exhaust-gas-driven turbocharger. This is achieved by using the hot exhaust gas to drive a turbine, which is permanently connected to a blower impeller. This pumps intake air into the engine at a fixed overpressure. The exhaust-gas-driven turbocharger has the following advantages:

- In motor sports, engine performance is increased to twice that of a normally aspirated engine if an exhaust-gas-driven turbocharger is used.
- For the same required maximum performance, an engine with an exhaust-gas-driven turbocharger can manage with a far smaller swept volume and lower engine speeds than a normally aspirated engine.
- The turbo-engine is far less susceptible to changes in atmospheric pressure, for example, when driving in the mountains.

The benefits described above are so striking that one is immediately tempted to ask what drawbacks the turbo has. Two are the sluggish response of the supercharger at low revs and, of course, the use of some highly complicated and expensive technology. So far as the engine itself is concerned, special attention must also be paid to the heightened mechanical stresses and their effects on the crank mechanism and the lubricating system. In view of the increased thermal stresses, the valves and pistons must be made of more heat-resistant material. Improvements in the engine cooling are also called for (intake air, water, and oil). The compression ratio must be progressively reduced the higher the degree of supercharging. Preparation of the mixture and ignition must also be adjusted to the special operating conditions of the turbocharger.

Only specially heat-resistant materials can be used in the area of the turbine impeller and the supercharger housing. When the engine is performing at the top end of its range, the temperature in and around those parts is approximately 1000°C. Due to the extremely high engine speeds of up to 150,000 rpm, the turbine and blower impeller must be extremely well balanced. The shaft must be especially well lubricated, and the turbine impellers must be made of the lightest, most heat-resistant, and most wear-resistant materials possible. All in all, no easy task for the manufacturer of turbochargers.

However, differences of opinion are now beginning to emerge among modern engine designers. There are clear signs that more and more designers and owners have decided in favor of the four-valve engine and have renounced the turbocharger because its well-known disadvantages impair its value as a drive unit for everyday cars. However, turbochargers and four-valve technology are not merely alternatives; when combined, they can provide optimum conditions for the very highest performance. This is certainly true of racing at the highest level—Formula 1 racing and rally prototypes.

With production cars, the technology associated with the combination of these two elements is restricted for the time being to the most expensive sports cars, since it is extremely difficult and costly to incorporate. As an example, the Porsche 959 and the Ferrari GTO, which fall into this category, have price tags of approximately 400,000 marks.

Only time will tell whether the volume car manufacturers will decide in favor of the one concept or the other, or even a combination of the two. At present, turbo-engines predominate where Mercedes tuners are concerned. The sole exception is AMG, with its V-8 four-valve engine. The combination of four-valve engine and turbocharger can be especially easily realized at a later stage in the 190 four-valve engine by adding a supercharger.

Work is proceeding at a feverish pace at Daimler-Benz anyway on the engine technology for the new S-class, which is due to be equipped with four-valve engines at the end of the 1980's at the latest. The current jewel in the Mercedes crown, however, is without doubt the 190 series (W 201).

Four-valve technology

In the Mercedes 190E 2.3-16, for example, the sporting power unit is based on a 2.3-liter four-cylinder engine that, in its standard form, develops 100 kW (136 hp).

Using the four-valve principle in a four-cylinder engine gives a total of sixteen valves; in optimized form, the engine produces 136 kW (185 hp). And this car is marketed by Daimler-Benz as a production model, if you please.

What are the special characteristics of this engine, then? In addition to its astonishing economy, it is the nature of the engine's performance that is so striking. As distinct from the turbocharger principle, in which full power output is available only at high engine speeds, say from 2,000 rpm upward, the sixteen-valve principle (four valves per cylinder) always gives optimum cylinder charging from low revs to high, resulting in a high level of torque. Slight loss of performance can, however, be seen in many four-valve engines in the zero to 1500 rpm range.

So what do sixteen valves mean to this engine? Each cylinder has two inlet and two outlet valves, which means a considerable increase in the breathing capacity of the power unit by comparison with the eight-valve version, since the intake air can flow into the cylinder via two inlets instead of just one. Within a given period of time, a greater quantity of mixture is fed to the cylinders, and the performance increases accordingly. On the other hand, the combustion air is rapidly removed from the cylinders via two outlet valves and an exhaust system of increased diameter, with a low back pressure. Naturally, timing, the length and

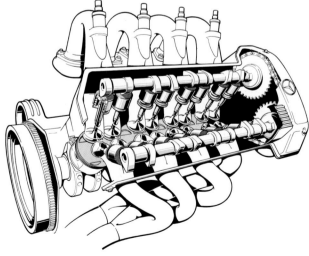

Mercedes 190E 2.3-16: cylinder head with two overhead camshafts and sixteen valves.

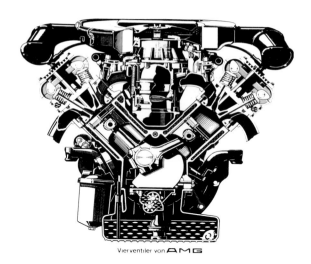

Vierventiler von **AMG**

Cutaway of the V-8 four-valve AMG engine.

exhaust-gas energy. The advantages of the four-valve engine lie in the high, smooth torque curve over the whole engine speed range, the excellent fuel consumption, and—of particular value in recent times—the very satisfactory exhaust emission values.

Admittedly, tuners (with just a few exceptions—Oettinger and Drake for VW and AMG for Daimler-Benz) are dependent on the manufacturers for bringing four-valve technology engines onto the market. Development costs are so enormously high that "normal" tuners could not possibly aspire to such heights, to say nothing of the technical know-how and engineering facilities involved.

arrangement of the intake and outlet pipes, and the piston of the plugs in a four-valve cylinder head all play a very important part. Here again, it is the sum of all these factors which leads to optimization of an engine.

Designers and technicians have known for a long time that four valves per cylinder provide the best opportunity of getting the maximum performance out of an engine. In spite of that, the use of four-valve technology has so far been largely restricted to racing cars, other competition cars, and a few exotic sports cars. The reason for this lies in the highly complicated construction, with a large number of moving parts, the amount of noise generated in the process, and the fairly high cost of maintenance. Furthermore, there are the high costs of manufacture in small numbers. Developments so far in the field of tuned production engines show quite clearly that output and torque are among the most important selling points in a power unit. The turbo-engine measures up to this requirement only in part because, although it usually has that well-known "kick in the back," it involves certain sacrifices at low revs and is always very heavy on fuel. The advantage of the exhaust-gas-driven turbine is that it can utilize part of the

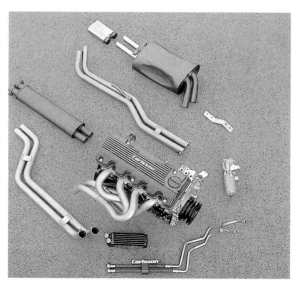

Motor tuning kit from Carlsson, based on the Mercedes 190E (W 201): The C24 power unit develops 126 kW (170 hp) at 6000 rpm, cubic capacity 2.4 liters, torque 228 Nm at 4000 rpm, top speed 220 km/h.

Chapter 7

Daimler-Benz—racing then and now

In order to fully understand the boom in modified Daimler-Benz models in the 1980's, it is important to remember the legendary Mercedes successes in motor racing. Without the image created by those racing cars, the outstanding reputation enjoyed today by cars bearing the three-pointed star would scarcely be thinkable.

Since the beginnings of the motor car one hundred years ago, Daimler-Benz cars have not merely shown themselves to be top-class products so far as quality, technology, and visual impact are concerned. They have also demonstrated their virtues of top-class performance coupled with reliability in that pitiless arena, the race track—an arena where second and third places count for nothing at all, and the first place for everything; where, in fact, despite all the skill and judgment displayed by the driver, it is the marque that triumphs, and not the person behind the wheel or the type of car. Victory becomes synonymous with the product itself, and the winning car is automatically considered to be the best.

Classification, ratings, handicapping systems that allow for several winners in the same race—nothing will change the way things are. Within a very few years at the latest, only the winner's name is remembered for the most part. Cognoscenti still remember highly creditable performances put up by those who did not quite make it to the line first, or the magnificent performances of cars only half as powerful as the "big boys," but the greater part of the prestige and glory belongs to the winner. This is all too clearly demonstrated by the sporting successes of the Mercedes racing cars and the fame that accompanies them and their counterparts on the highways and byways.

Even in the early days of the motor car, there were enough people around who were ambitious and eager to prove that they were the fastest. The so-called competition vehicles of the time were mostly standard everyday "carriages," often built in series production, although this term cannot in any way be equated with series production as we know it today, especially since every car produced at the time was modified to suit its owner's taste and requirements. In the early days of motor sport, the competitions held were more in the nature of long-distance road races, intended to demonstrate that, after only a few years, these evil-smelling, gas-driven horseless carriages were perfectly capable of competing with horses.

The date of the first excursion in a motor car was pinpointed as 1886, when Berta Benz made the trip from Mannheim to Pforzheim. Although this date may seem a little arbitrary, there can be no doubt about the date of the first competition held for motor cars, advertised on December 19, 1893, as due to the run from Paris to Rouen on July 22, 1894. This distance was a not inconsiderable 126 kilometers and the event was organized by the Paris newspaper *Le Petit Journal*.

In this event, it was not so much the speed of the competitors—a maximum time of eight and one-half hours was allowed to complete the course—as the reliability of the vehicles taking part. This was further underlined by the rules drawn up for the event, in which it was stated

Daimler's "motor coach" of 1886 illustrates admirably the earliest days of motoring.

that the first prize of 5,000 francs would be awarded to the competitor whose vehicle was "not hazardous," "easy for its driver to manage," and "not too costly to maintain." Only "horseless carriages" were allowed to take part.

Though it was barely ten years since that first excursion, more than one hundred vehicles were entered. They included vehicles running on different types of petroleum products, as well as electric cars and "steamers"—in fact, anything that could be used to produce horsepower, except the genuine thing.

Of the one hundred or so vehicles entered, just twenty-one were allowed to start, the rest having been weeded out in advance by the ultra-strict race organizers. The actual competition took place on July 22, 1894, as planned, and did in fact develop into a race. Although times were not taken into account in adjudicating, there was an almighty tussle to see who could get across the line first.

The official joint winners were judged to be the marques Peugeot and Panhard-Levasseur, which *Le Petit Journal* judged to be "handy and light." These cars already had German hearts, their engines having been built by Gottlieb Daimler in Stuttgart.

Basically, this is where the legend started. Whereas Peugeot and Panhard-Levasseur gradually moved toward rather simpler workaday cars that were no longer capable of creating a sporting image, the Daimler and, later, Daimler-Benz products were able to maintain their position at the top, both in everyday motoring and in racing.

At the beginning of the twentieth century, the Daimler sports car—renamed Mercedes after the daughter of the Austrian nobleman and importer, Emil Jellinek—appeared on the scene and dominated it for years, despite the most strenuous efforts on the part of French and Italian manufacturers, such as Peugeot, Panhard, Renault, Fiat, and Itala. However, other long-since-forgotten marques, such as de Dietrich, Darracq, Brasier, Hotchkiss, Gregoire, Berliet, and Clement-Bayard, also registered surprise wins and caused many a stir.

Between World War I and World War II, Ettore Bugatti's cars appeared on the scene like a breath of fresh air and frequently succeeded in pushing Mercedes off the winner's podium. But before then, shortly before World War I broke out, came the age of the giant car—the dinosaurs of the automobile world. Carl Benz was probably responsible for the creation of these monsters. In 1908, he constructed the world speed record car, the Blitzen (Lightning) Benz, from a successful racing car that ran in the Grand Prix des ACF (French Automobile Club). Whereas the GP car of 1908 had a capacity of 12.5 liters and developed about 110 kW (150 hp) at 1500 rpm, which secured it second place behind a Mercedes, the Blitzen Benz had a capacity of 21.5 liters and developed 147 kW (200 hp) at 1600 rpm.

With this car, the 200 km/h "sound barrier" was broken for the first time on November 8, 1909. The French driver Victor Hemery clocked precisely 202.691 km/h at Brooklands. It was not until May 17, 1922, that this record was broken, by an Englishman, K. Lee Guiness, who attained a speed of 215.244 km/h.

The last important race before the outbreak of World War I was also won by a Mercedes. The Grand Prix de France, on July 5, 1914, was won by Lautenschlager in a 4.5-liter Mercedes that developed 85 kW (115 hp) and set up an average speed, sensational given the conditions of those days, of 105 km/h, which Lautenschlager kept up, driving entirely on his own, for more than seven hours.

Special highlights of racing during the late 1920's, when large cars dominated many of the races, were the competition cars derived from the standard S-model Mercedes. An S-type sports car driven by Otto Merz, for example, won the first Grand Prix, held on the newly completed Nurburgring in 1927.

The revolutionary technology of its six-cylinder supercharged 6.8-liter engine was largely derived from this series and undoubtedly helped the road model to achieve worldwide fame, due to its fantastic successes.

Further developments based on the S-type, namely the SS of 1928 with 7.1-liter capacity and the famous SSK, introduced in 1929 with a 7.1-liter supercharged engine developing 165 kW (225 hp), continued the run of racing successes. The name of the most successful driver associated with them no doubt added greatly to the prestige and the image of the name Mercedes—Rudolf Caracciola. With his giant, sluggish standard SSK, he took up the apparently hopeless struggle against the Alfa Romeos and Maseratis—specially designed for formula racing—which were as quick as weasels and almost as powerful as the SSK, and above all against the all-conquering Bugattis.

Among other successes, Caracciola drove his car to victory in the German Grand Prix on the Nurburgring in 1931 and, in the same year, in the Mille Miglia, the most important sports car road race of its day, run over 1700 kilometers nonstop from Brescia to Rome and back again. But after that, the lean years set in with a vengeance for German racing. Even Caracciola left for Alfa Romeo and continued to dominate the scene, together with Maserati and Bugatti.

However, German racing cars dominated the scene all the more emphatically in the years 1934 to 1939, not least because that was the express wish of the political leaders of the time, who saw in motor racing an expression and potent symbol of the superiority of German technology. The "signboards" that they used to advertise those ideas went by the name of Auto-Union and Daimler-Benz.

Once again, it was the Daimler-Benz cars that managed to keep their nose out in front of the others, although it was Auto-Union that enjoyed the greater sympathy and political support.

The years 1934 to 1937 were the years of the famous 750-kg formula car races, in which, apart from the maximum car weight, only the minimum length of the race was laid down—500 km. The choice of fuel was unrestricted, so the petroleum and chemical industries concocted all manner of devilish mixtures to power the cars, the main secret of which lay in the internal cooling of the engine; this increased efficiency, and with it performance.

The Daimler racing car of this period was the W 25. The counterpart produced by the Auto-Union (created a few years earlier from the ailing Audi, DKW, Horch and Wanderer companies) was the very first mid-engined racing car produced that was worth taking seriously. The designer was Ferdinand Porsche and the engine

had no fewer than sixteen cylinders. The Mercedes W 25, on the other hand, was a fairly conventional eight-cylinder front-engined car. In spite of that, it managed to keep up with Ferdinand Porsche's revolutionary Type A for much of the way in a duel between two prestigious marques; in the struggle for the world road racing record, with the eyes of the whole world on him, Caracciola managed to clock 317.5 km/h with this car.

The slight inferiority experienced by Daimler-Benz in 1934 left them no peace and, after certain refinements had been made, the W 25 quite clearly set the tone in 1935. It owed this in particular to its superior specific output of no less than 79 kW per liter of capacity (108 hp/liter), whereas all its competitors had to manage with between 55 and 63 kW/liter (75–80 hp/liter).

Nineteen hundred and thirty-six was the year of Bernd Rosemeyer and the Auto-Union. Rosemeyer, a former motorcycle racer, dominated almost unchallenged all the Grand Prix events. Only once did Caracciola manage to win with the W 125.

Mercedes-Benz SSK streamlined model with Otto Merz at the wheel.

Daimler-Benz did not give up, of course, and preparations were made to get back at Auto-Union in the struggle for prestige in the 1937 season. The result was the W 125, perhaps the best-known racing car of the years between the wars and, in most cases, the oldest "silver arrow" known to the present-day generation of Mercedes racing drivers. With 5.6 liters capacity, a power output of about 450 kW (650 hp), and the quite phenomenal specific engine output for that time and class of engine of 84 kW/liter (114 hp/liter), it was the most powerful formula racing car of all time until the mid-1960's. Only then was this incredible output surpassed by the cars built for the Indianapolis 500.

It was only at the beginning of the 1980's that the Formula 1 racing cars, directly comparable with the Auto-Union and Mercedes cars, managed with the aid of turbocharged engines to squeeze outputs of 515 kW (700 hp) and more from swept volumes of three liters. The size of the achievement, given the conditions prevailing at the time, can be appreciated more fully if one considers that tires often had to be changed more than five times during the course of a 500 km race. As a result of the enormous motive forces involved and the crazy speeds at which cars cornered on the tracks of that period, the materials were simply not up to it and tires would last about 100 km at the most.

In 1937, just one year after Bernd Rosemeyer and Auto-Union had held sway in such convincing fashion, Mercedes was once again king of the circuits with the W 125. Not only the magnificent Caracciola but also Hermann Lang and Manfred von Brauchitsch recorded their names

"Most powerful racing car of all time" was the word in 1937: Mercedes-Benz 750-kg formula racing car (W 125).

on the list of GP winners. The Mercedes star shone again everywhere.

Even a change in the rules in 1938 could do nothing to shake the dominance of Mercedes. Quite the reverse! As a result of the tragic death of Bernd Rosemeyer—he crashed at over 400 km/h during a world speed record attempt on the autobahn near Frankfurt—the only serious competition had lost their most talented and courageous driver. With the W 154, Daimler-Benz dominated the new three-liter formula races: three-liter V-12 engine, 345 kW (470 hp) at 7800 rpm, 155 kW/liter (157 hp/liter), twin superchargers, four valves per cylinder. Caracciola, driving Daimler-Benz, became European champion—which equates to the world champion in modern Formula 1 racing—for the third time, following his successes in 1935 and 1937.

In 1939, the last racing season before World War II, Daimler-Benz introduced another new racing car, the W 163. The most outstanding technical feature of this car was its experimental fuel injection, which did not become common-place in racing engines until the 1950's. The W 163 was also superior to all comers. Hermann Lang collected his European championship title in this car. Its wonderful victories and clear all-round supremacy at the highest level of motor racing left an indelible mark on the road cars of the Stuttgart marque between the two World Wars.

Anyone who thought anything of himself at all, and had enough money or influence, drove a Mercedes—not the least of the reasons for this being the aura of technical excellence reflected in its successes on the race track. The sequence of Daimler-Benz successes was then interrupted by World War II and the period of reconstruction that followed.

Finally, the legendary gullwing sports car, the Mercedes 300 SL, notched up its first successes, succeeding at the first attempt against the Maseratis and Alfa Romeos, which had become accustomed to success, and the first cars produced by Enzo Ferrari. The way back into Formula 1 racing was smoothed by doctoring the

Mercedes-Benz racing car of 1939 (Tripolis) with V-8 engine and 254 hp (W 163).

engine of the gullwing car for competition purposes. The three-liter direct-injection engine, cut down to 2.5-liter capacity to satisfy the rules but representing the very peak of technical excellence, took its place in the post-war silver arrow W 196 in 1954–55.

Daimler-Benz's decision to take up Formula 1 racing again was made in 1952 when the 300 SL prototypes won the premier sports car race in the world, Le Mans, at their first attempt. The whole racing world was immediately reminded of the unforgettable racing successes of the prewar years and knew at once: The enforced lay-off of the war years had done nothing to dent the technical excellence of Daimler-Benz's cars. They came back, they saw, they conquered at a stroke.

Daimler's engineers had a few brilliant ideas that ensured their superiority over all comers for years to come. In particular, there were three refinements:

- direct fuel injection, which made for pretty hard running but produced maximum performance
- desmodromic valve operation—positive valve control by means of a C-shaped lever element— for maximum speed without valve bounce
- a streamlined body with covered wheels and considerably improved C_d value for high-speed stretches

In the 1954 and 1955 racing seasons, Daimler-Benz dominated top class racing to an almost frightening degree; the prizes for sports car races fell to the 300SL and 300 SLR, while Formula 1 races went to the W 196.

The Formula 1 cars, for example, notched up twelve wins from fifteen starts; on seven of these occasions they took the first two places, on one the first three, and on another the first four!

At the end of 1955, Daimler-Benz withdrew from both types of racing, and to this day the

Mercedes-Benz Formula 1 racing car W 196 of 1954, with 2.5-liter eight-cylinder engine and 280 hp at 8500 rpm, direct fuel injection, desmodromic valve gear, weight 640 kg. Drivers: Fangio, Kling, Hermann, Moss.

Mercedes-Benz W 196 (with streamlined body) of 1954, engine data as previously, weight 680 kg. In some cases, these cars ran on a special mixture of alcohol and benzene; it was so aggressive that it could not be left overnight in the tank.

Mercedes-Benz sports car 300 SL of 1954. The 3-liter six-cylinder engine developed 175 hp at 5200 rpm, giving the car a top speed of 240 km/h.

company's position has not changed. The management sought to justify the decision by drawing attention to the dual responsibilities and the greatly increased load that fell on their best designers and technicians as a result of their involvement in both racing and production cars. However, the principal reason was probably the terrible accident that occurred at Le Mans in 1955, when the French driver Pierre Levegh, through no fault of his own, caused the death of eighty-five spectators when he was involved in a collision immediately in front of the stand and was thrown straight into it. He was driving a Mercedes 300 SLR. Daimler-Benz immediately withdrew all works cars from sports car races. In October of the same year came the announcement that Formula 1 racing would also be discontinued.

In spite of all the urging and pleading by the public, Daimler-Benz has not been able to commit to entering any works cars in any form of racing. So far, any attempt made was either half-hearted or merely in a supporting role. Whether it was the entry of the 300 SE in circuit racing and rallying for touring cars in the early 1960's or the later entry of the 280E (W 123) and 450 SL (R 107) in rallying, each time the Daimler-Benz fans waited for total commitment of a works team. But each time, after a promising start, it all petered out again, despite very considerable successes in the Monte Carlo Rally, the East African Safari, and the European Touring Car Championships.

When Daimler-Benz finally signed up the best German rally driver, Walter Rohrl, as a factory driver after a few noteworthy successes with the 280E and 450 SL, many people thought that

Mercedes-Benz sports car 300 SLR of 1955 with three-liter eight-cylinder engine and 310 hp at 7400 rpm, top speed approximately 290 km/h. Drivers: Moss, Fangio, Kling.

64

AMG racing touring car, then . . .

. . . AMG racing model (Group A) of the present day, based on the Mercedes 190 E 2.3-16. The 16-valve racing engine develops more than 230 hp at about 7500 rpm, maximum torque is given as 255 Nm at 6000 rpm, acceleration 0-100 km/h in less than 6 seconds, top speed about 250 km/h. ➡

Carlsson racing Model (Group A), based on Mercedes 190 (W 201).

this was it. But far from it—the contract was canceled, and Rohrl had to look for another boss.

Although—or possibly because—Daimler-Benz production cars have acquired an increasing reputation as high-quality but somewhat conservative and comfortable cars since the end of the 1950's, when the 300 SL was discontinued after the withdrawal from racing, no one has forgotten the sporting successes of the marque and the absolute technical superiority the cars enjoyed on the race tracks.

Perhaps this is the reason the management is holding back—afraid, perhaps, that they would be unable to fulfill the enormous expectations that would attend any works entry.

Tuning Mercedes cars for the road has made possible postproduction modification of the characteristics of the production car in a sporting direction. With the introduction of the 190 E 2.3-16 (four-valve), Daimler-Benz has created an opportunity for these same tuners to bring back to it some of the glory it once knew on the racing track—or at least to make a start in that direction.

The next stage has already been sighted—the first top-class racing cars with a Daimler-Benz V-8 engine and turbocharger or twin turbocharger are already being put through their paces by the Swiss firm of Sauber and the Lotec company. Maybe this represents a fresh start for the three-pointed star, a first step on the ladder to renewed racing success.

Chapter 8

Pros and cons

Anyone who has spoken to responsible people from Daimler-Benz will have noticed the strange ambiguity—they never express a clear opinion for or against when the conversation turns to the "metal-bashing artists" and "engine tweakers."

On the one hand, there is the conviction, nurtured on a daily diet of excellence, that Daimler-Benz products cannot be improved on, either visually or technically. On the other hand, they look on tuners and stylists as clients who can help them sell their products, rather than selling those of their competitors. One or two of them will occasionally even admit that a 190 that has been lowered and fitted with wider wheels is quite an eyecatcher—in spite of the factory-supplied four-valve-engined 190.

They will also admit that, on the technical side, they have very cordial relations with a number of selected tuning and styling firms. This is especially true of those firms prepared to nurture the new 190 E 2.3-16 to grow and flourish at the expense of the BMW, Daimler-Benz's main rival from Munich, in the hope that there might soon be another "starlet" visible in the racing firmament, even if only with unofficial works support—or possibly even a fully-blown star in the form of the big new four-valve cars of 3.0 to 5.6 liter capacity.

The resolve of the Daimler-Benz management to keep out of racing altogether has so far weakened to the extent that there is now a very sizable book full of homologated parts, intended to get the 190 into competitive order for the race track. There are such goodies available as a new front end for the low-slung racing cars, special racing brakes, axle joints, and camshafts. However, there is no actual cooperation between the two sides—just plenty of work for the tuners and stylists.

These parts are sold exclusively by the branch factory in Kassel, which is well known from earlier racing days for its support of the *Scuderia Kassel* (Kassel Stable), a sports car racing association in which Holger Bohne notched up notable rallying and rallycross successes with the 280 E (W 123) and further rallying successes with the 450 SLC.

If the "boys from Kassel" were merely tolerated at the time, they are now seen as semi-pros from the past and made very welcome.

Leaving the race track aside and turning to road cars, there is a more or less marked divergence of opinion between Daimler-Benz and the tuning and styling fraternity. Whereas Daimler-Benz takes a "sensible" approach, and considers that the four-valve 190 engine has sufficient potential for the entire program, the tuners take an entirely different view. So far as styling and tuning ex-works is concerned, Daimler-Benz offers nothing more than the chassis and bodywork parts from the four-valve 190 for the standard W 201 models. It goes something like this: the 190 diesel or two-valve gas engine car owner has a choice among these items purchased exclusively from Daimler-Benz factory spare parts services: front spoiler and wing; front spoiler, rocker panels, rear apron, and wing, chassis and bodywork kit. These must then be entered in the appropriate vehicle documents. Any other combination, for example, chassis without spoiler parts or with spoiler only, is not allowed.

The production version of the Mercedes 190 E 2.3-16, as delivered ex-works, can be lowered by 15 mm, that is, 30 mm lower in all than the standard model of the 190. That is the only modification directly sanctioned by the factory. When the question of tuning arises, then the answer is a blunt no, so there will be no sixteen-valve engines in the standard 190.

Later modifications to all the other series, the middle-range, S-class, and the SL, are strictly taboo. The prospects for any change in that direction are very slim indeed.

Styling parts, so one hears, might follow for the W 124, but only if there are technical benefits in terms of ride stability without affecting the suitability of the car for everyday motoring. Such a solution is possible in principle, but involves a great deal of effort and would be very expensive.

No bodywork parts can be expected from the factory for the S class, and so far as the new SL (R 129) is concerned, there is the possibility that it will not need them anyway, nor require them for aerodynamic reasons, as is the case with the 190, where the ride safety of this sixteen-valve-engined car has been noticeably improved by modifications to the chassis and bodywork.

Engine tuning is viewed in a skeptical light on principle, since "enhanced performance" is available ex-works anyway (for example, up to 136 kW (185 hp) in the case of the 190, and recently up to 200 kW (272 hp) in the case of the S class) insofar as within each series there are models with different performance levels, the most powerful of which has more than enough performance to offer—in the eyes of the Daimler-Benz technicians, anyway.

The tuners, it must be said, are of a different opinion on this point. They are able to offer, on all Daimler-Benz cars, engines of greater capacity, six-cylinder and eight-cylinder engines for the smaller series, turbochargers, mechanical superchargers and, in the case of AMG, a four-valve V-8 engine.

The tuner's customer pays for the pleasure of driving a car that is superior to the supposedly more powerful—or at least equally powerful—production car by making sacrifices in the suitability of the vehicle for everyday motoring, in its service life, comfort, and reliability, all of which features have been optimized so lovingly and at such expense at the factory.

The new laws on car exhaust emissions, which come into force in 1988, may well give the tuner a few headaches, if only because they lay down very stringent emission levels for larger-engined cars, which can only be achieved at the present time with the aid of a catalyzer. This will lead to a vehicle's registration becoming automatically void the moment the timings are changed, that is, if another camshaft is fitted. One-off approvals will be very time-consuming and costly due to the comprehensive cycle of tests required.

Whatever the reasons may be, Daimler-Benz is going for output. Four-valve technology—currently much favored by Daimler-Benz designers and technicians—will no doubt be introduced for all series, as it has been for the 190, not only because it provides a basis for increasing output without all the usual problems but also because it results in quicker, more even, and thus cleaner combustion.

Since the factory is not hell-bent on achieving maximum performance—for example, 136 kW (185 hp) is considered adequate for the compact 190, about 176 kW (240 hp) for the middle-range W 124, and 200 kW (272 hp) for the S class—modest increases of the order of twenty to thirty percent are entirely feasible if the competition forces them into it. As a result, the use of turbochargers or mechanical superchargers to pep up the performance of gas engines is not a subject that Daimler-Benz is considering at all.

This latter question is reserved for the diesel—and possibly an evolutionary series of compact or middle-range Mercedes cars for racing homologation—always provided that the international racing body, FISA, does not bar the use of turbo-engines in order to put a stop to the positive explosion in engine performance figures that has taken place in recent years.

Styling Garage: Gullwing car based on Mercedes sports car. Strictly speaking, the star should have been removed from the grille of this car produced by the former SGS company: All that glitters may not be gold.

So, the tuners will be hard at work until 1988 on refining Daimler-Benz power units, after which it remains to be seen what the performance-at-all-cost motorist will do: buy four-valve production engines or. . . .

Neither are the Daimler people all that enthusiastic about styling changes—they occasionally take delight in exercising their right to forbid the use of the three-pointed star to set the "seal of approval" on a new styling variant. Whereas the technicians quite properly point out that the addition, for instance, of wider wheels to increase the track width can have a

negative affect on the wishbone mountings, bearings, suspension, level control, and brakes, the factory legal department will quite simply say, "A Mercedes that has been modified in any essential detail is not a Mercedes any more and may not use the Mercedes star. End of message!"

This means that the trademarks, the three-pointed star and the Daimler-Benz flourishes, everything that characterizes a Mercedes car, must be removed. Since the trademark identifies the manufacturer, everything added on or converted by the tuning and styling companies would count as a Mercedes product!

As the manufacturer (and Daimler-Benz is not alone in this—it applies to the other car manufacturers as well) plays a fiduciary role and is intent on maintaining its image, it forbids tuning and styling companies to use its trademark. In such cases, the company carrying out the modification immediately has to sign a negative covenant that states, in effect, that if it should persist in using the trademark, on each occasion it so uses it it will be liable for a hefty fine—probably a few thousand marks—which would go to swell Daimler-Benz's coffers.

Examples of cases in which such measures have to be taken are major modifications to bodywork or engine, wheelbase extensions, conversions of limousines or coupes into convertibles, addition or removal of major portions of bodywork (such as wing doors), or increase of the capacity of the engine. It is also well known that the factory forbids the use of the three-pointed star if SEC-style hoods are installed on models of other series. Such modifications cannot of themselves be legally forbidden; the manufacturer merely has the right to insist on the removal of its trademark.

However, this only affects the conversion for profit or the trade in general. That is, the restraint is applied only to anyone who carries out such conversions or modifications for a monetary or other consideration or who trades in such converted or modified products—not exclusively automobile parts but also such simple things as cigarette lighters, key rings, or T-shirts. In all such cases, the trademark may be used only with the manufacturer's express approval.

The final step in this sequence occurs when it operates in reverse. The purchaser that is, the end user, owner, or driver, may put the star and the trademark back again in their original places. So a Mercedes car that in the eyes of the Daimler-Benz legal eagles is no longer a Mercedes car can suddenly turn into a Mercedes car again, at least externally, for all to see. That this cannot exactly gladden the hearts of the management in Stuttgart will be seen from the following incident, which actually occurred.

When an "enhanced" S-class Mercedes broke in two in the middle because it had been inexpertly extended, the resulting headlines in the paper did not read "Styling company XYZ slips up when extending Mercedes" but "Mercedes breaks in two—passengers injured." It is not difficult to appreciate that this is no joke for Daimler-Benz and can do nothing but harm its reputation, especially since the name of the company that carried out the conversion is not even mentioned in the report. Everyone unaware of the full facts would automatically assume that the car was in its original condition, as delivered from the factory.

Names and abbreviations patented by Daimler-Benz may also not be misused by the tuning or styling companies. The names in ques-

Trasco: Imperial sedan based on S-class Mercedes.

tion are, for example, Mercedes, Daimler-Benz, Mercedes-Benz; the abbreviations include SE, SEL, SEC, SL, and SLC.

Firms that restrict themselves to minor styling packages are exempt from all such legal niceties. A "minor styling package" is taken by Daimler-Benz's legal department to mean for example, a simple spoiler kit, consisting perhaps of front spoiler, rocker panels, rear apron, rear spoiler or wing, wheels, springs, shock absorbers, and tires. And these, of course, only if they are stylistically inoffensive and technically sound, that is, already have TÜV approval.

Even fender extensions, for example, no longer come under the heading of minor styling modifications. Tuners therefore have rather less room to maneuver than they would like and take

every opportunity to display their products at fairs and exhibitions, having them photographed for advertising purposes, always without the star, its place being taken by some other badge, such as the initials ABC, SGS (for Styling Garage), KS (Koenig Specials), or simply a big "T" (for Trasco) on the radiator. And then it does not matter any more whether the SEC grille is installed in an SEC, an SEL, or a 190. That simplifies matters somewhat.

And when the stylists and tuners do get their hands on the cars—because they cannot get them just like that from the factory—then they can drill and punch and screw and weld to their heart's content. The only thing that matters then is that they have a customer who will like the resulting product and will buy it.

Chapter 9

Tuners and body stylists

Never before—and on no other marque—have so many tuning and styling specialists practiced their craft as are now working on conversions of the current Daimler-Benz model range.

The S class current at the time, the top of the Daimler-Benz range, was the spur that induced AMG, Brabus, and Lorinser to undertake wholesale mechanical and styling modifications to Mercedes models.

The compact Mercedes (W201), the 190 series, was a not unwelcome addition and, after a few initial problems, proved to be the "honeypot" that attracted the attention of tuners and stylists of every kind. Never before has the styling and tuning fraternity contributed so much to the image of a base model as in the case of the 190 series.

All of a sudden, the broad, low, wedge-shaped compact Mercedes appeared on the road and attracted immediate attention. Even when standing still, it appears to be bursting with energy and raring to go, despite the fact that it has a perfectly standard engine under the hood.

The Cinderellas of this period were the older middle-range series W123 and SL family sports cars (R107). While the SL is still awaiting the arrival of its successor, currently undergoing exhaustive trials, the W123 has already witnessed the introduction of the new Daimler-Benz middle-range W124 designed to take its place—much to the delight of the stylists and tuners. They fell all over the new model the moment it was available, hoping that it would bring the crock of gold they had all been waiting for while honing their skills on the smaller and larger model ranges.

Whether their expectations will be fulfilled or not remains to be seen. In spite of the obvious demand, the cake must be cut into so many slices that there may well be nothing but crumbs left over for some. The old adage "Too many cooks spoil the broth" could also prove to be all too true, and there could be a certain amount of redundancy among the "cooks."

The following summary chart gives an overview of the activities of the individual tuning and styling firms that will enable the reader who has already decided on a certain model with specific modifications to target his search more accurately.

This list of selected firms has been supplemented by their addresses (in the Appendix) to which the reader can turn for special parts, for example, for older Mercedes-Benz models. It should be pointed out at this juncture that the firms concerned could add to their programs at any time. However, this should not significantly affect the summary. If they are already in contact with any of these firms, readers will no doubt automatically receive details of any changes in their programs.

Key
O, visual styling: internal and external bodywork changes—for example, spoilers, and extended fenders—without any major modifications to the original bodywork and chassis.

	W 201	W 123	W 124	W 116	W 126	W 107	G
ABC	O, K, F		O, F		O, K, F	O, F	
Air Press	O						
AMG	O, F, M	O, F, M	O, F, M	O, F, M	O, F, M	O, F, M	O, F, M
APAL	S						
ASS	O						
bb Auto					K		
BBS	O, F	O, F	O, F		O, F	F	
Benny S					O, K, F		
Bickel					O		
Brabus	O, F, M	O, F, M	O, F, M	F, M	O, F, M	O, F, M	
Brinkmeyer		O	O				
Car Design Schacht	O, F, M		O, F, M				
Carlsson	O, F, M		O, F, M				
Caruna					K		
D + W	O, F	O, F	O, F		O, F	O, F	
Daimler-Benz	O, F						
Duchatelet	O, F		O, F		O, F, K		
ES	O, F						
Gemballa					O, F		
GFG		K, F, M	S		O, K, F, M		
Haslbeck			O				
HF	O		O		O	O	
Isdera	S				S		
Kamei	O				O		
Kodiak					S		
Koenig Specials			O, F, M		O, F, M	O, F, M	
Konig					O		
Kugok					O, F, M		
Lorenz + Rankl	F, M				S		
Lorinser	O, F, M	O, F	O, F	O, F	O, F	O, F	O, F
Lotec	O, F, M		O, F, M		O, F		
MAE	O, F	O, F	O, F		O, F		
MTS	O, F	O	O, F				
Oettinger	M						
Ronny Coach					O, K		
Sbarro					K, S		
Schulz	O, K, F, M	O, K	O, F, M		O, K, F	O	
SKV	K						
Styling Garage	O, K		K		O, K, S		
Taifun	O						
Trasco					O, K		
Turbo-Motors	M	M	M		M	M	
Vestatec	O		O				
Zender	O, F	O	O		O, K	O	

K, body conversions: wheelbase extensions and major conversion work on original body, such as conversion of limousines and hard-top style cars into convertibles and coupes.

S, special models: completely new cars without reference to original bodywork and, in some cases, without reference to original chassis.

F, chassis modifications: modifications to the chassis, such as lowering the suspension, widening the track, and so on, not necessarily in conjunction with styling changes to the bodywork.

M, engine tuning: modifications to the engine designed to increase performance.

Here is a brief look at the company philosophy and the overall program of the firms listed. Where necessary, details include excerpts from the company's own literature, reproduced in unedited form. (Individual tuning and styling measures are described in detail in the following chapters, model by model.)

ABC

This relatively young company has set itself two main target areas: On the one hand are conventional spoilers with restrained styling on Daimler-Benz models, and on the other are extremely wide conversions and expensive convertibles.

The extremely comprehensive conventional program for the styling of Daimler-Benz cars extends from simple front spoilers (under panel) through wings and fender extensions to the new trunk lids with breakaway foils, SEC hoods, and interior styling.

The Gotti wheels in ABC's program are a speciality. These are available for all current Daimler-Benz limousines.

In the same way, convertibles are built on the base of any of the Mercedes limousines, as well as special wide versions with extremely wide wheels. The middle- and upper-range Daimler-Benz models are fitted with 345/35 tires at the rear, while the compact Mercedes runs on quite respectable 285/40 tires. The corresponding rear parts, that is, the wings, are of a suitable radius and size. The only exception to this is the wide version of the compact Mercedes; the fender extensions here are fairly restrained. In the S class, ABC produces wheelbase extensions

for the imperial sedan. Except where necessary for the wide versions, engine and chassis modifications play only a secondary role.

Since the company's first public appearance at the IAA in Frankfurt in 1983, its philosophy can be summed up in their own words: "ABC will provide the driver who has a weakness for motor sport, elegance, and harmony, with a very special car." That anything special has a price goes without saying.

Air Press

This company first appeared on the scene as a styling company and has recently entered the market with a program for the compact Mercedes 190.

AMG

It is not without good reason that the words "engine construction" point to both the company's history and its philosophy. In the early days, when A stood for Hans-Werner Aufrecht, M for Erhard Melcher, and G for Grossaspach, near Stuttgart, the company dedicated itself to engine construction—not only for motor racing, but also for road cars.

In the year of its foundation, 1967, this was quite sensational. No other firm had dared to commit itself so fervently to modifying Daimler-Benz limousines for racing purposes. AMG did just that, in the shape of the legendary 6.3-liter version. And not without success, either.

Erhard Melcher left the company in 1970, and in 1976, the seat of the company was moved to Affalterbach, close by. At the same time, the meteoric rise of the tuning specialist Hans-Werner Aufrecht began and, as almost no other person in the field, he made the tuning and styling of Mercedes cars what it is today—assisted in no small measure by their racing successes.

The mechanical modification and tuning were soon followed by styling changes, some of which, such as front spoilers and fender extensions, were a necessary corollary to the technical refinements.

In the meantime, AMG, seen as a whole, probably has the most comprehensive program of styling and tuning parts of any company in the business. They can provide bodywork, interior, chassis, and engine tuning kits for all current and many discontinued Mercedes-Benz models.

As Hans-Werner Aufrecht said of the company, "As a result of their long years of experience with Daimler-Benz cars, AMG have the sort of know-how which enables them to take on the most comprehensive, even bizarre, customer modifications and to carry them out to the customer's complete satisfaction."

The only areas where AMG has no desire to tread—no doubt a shrewd move, seen in the context of the company's philosophy—are major conversions of models of various different kinds into convertibles, and other jobs of this kind.

Apal

This Belgian manufacturer of buggies and replica cars, based on the VW, is in the process of building his own coupe, the mechanical parts for which are taken from the compact Mercedes 190 series.

ASS

Like many other, ASS, a manufacturer of sports car seats, is keen to profit from the general trend toward individual styling and equipment. Among other cars, they have taken on the conversion of a Daimler-Benz model, the compact Mercedes W 201.

bb Auto

Hidden behind this name is none other than the firm b + b (founded by Buchmann).

In addition to work with Porsche and VW models, Buchmann expends much time and love on two models derived from Daimler-Benz cars: The first of these is the experimental BB-CW 311 sports car, which owes a great deal visually to the former Wankel experimental car produced by Daimler-Benz and destined for the top-flight category of sports cars. The other is the so far unique convertible version of the SED coupe with an original hard top, which breaks down into several pieces and is opened and closed by motors. The whole assembly is known as the Magic Top, which sounds suitable! Another fea-

ture well worth mentioning in bb Auto cars is the digital infoboard, which takes the place of the conventional instruments, even in Daimler-Benz cars.

What, then, is the philosophy of bb Autos? Buchmann claims that he has added "creativity and attractiveness" to the sonorous quality concept "Made in Germany." A pity that the company got into financial difficulties in 1986.

BBS

The firm of BBS, in Schiltach, is nearly synonymous with wheels. No other company has succeeded in bringing onto the market a product that is of such typical design and that speaks for itself in quite the same way as the BBS lattice wheel. The high reputation that this wheel enjoys undoubtedly derives in great measure from the enormous investment BBS has made in sports racing—and their total commitment to it.

In addition to that, BBS also supply chassis kits, predominantly for BMW, Daimler-Benz, and VW models.

Where Daimler-Benz is concerned, BBS restricts itself to spoiler kits for the 190 series and the new middle-range 200-300 (W 124) models.

BBS is of the opinion that individuality, and thus quality, are in demand—"in contrast to the philosophy of mass production." And BBS acts accordingly.

Benny S

The first fruits of this team are as charming as its name—a thoroughly boisterous S-class coupe by the name of PanAm. There is also a convertible version and digital instruments.

Brabus

Along with AMG, Brabus is one of the few manufacturers that can offer a complete styling and tuning program for new and older Daimler-Benz models. The firm was set up in 1978 but did not produce any spectacular results until they succeeded in 1985 in setting up, in their own words, "a new world record for C_d in production cars," using a new middle-range Mercedes (W

124) equipped with spoiler parts from their own serial production (C_d = 0.2625).

In recent times, Brabus has taken up mechanical turbosupercharging in addition to conventional engine tuning.

The philosophy of the company dictates that a car should be "sporting and elegant, without attracting immediate attention."

Brinkmeyer

Brinkmeyer, manufacturers of spoiler kits for various makes and models, also makes construction kits for the new and old Daimler-Benz middle-range (W 123/W 124) cars.

Carlsson

Ingvar Carlsson, a rally driver from Sweden, founded the firm of Carlsson Motorsport in 1984, together with the former BMW tuner Andreas Hartge.

True to the company philosophy, which is "to take an active part in motor-sports in order to exploit the experience gained on a commercial basis," the firm primarily developed tuning kits for the compact and middle-range Mercedes engines. In parallel, it also developed body styling kits for the same models.

Carlsson's star performer is the compact Mercedes 190 (W 201) with a 5.0-liter engine and an output of 272 hp.

Caruna

"If people were aware of the potency of the Mercedes engine, then much of the tuning carried out on Mercedes cars would simply not take place."

This is the opinion of the Swiss family firm of Schill, founded in 1964. In order to live up to this high ideal, the firm of Caruna practices considerable self-restraint and predominantly builds only a Targa variant of the SEC coupe and a very stylish four-door convertible-limousine, based on the S-class Mercedes.

D + W

D + W is, in its own words, "Number 1 in Germany for sporting car accessories." The letters stand for the owners' names, Detlef Sokowicz and Werner Bauer. After dealing for a long time in other people's products, the bosses decided to produce their own. And what was the best line open to them, given the available sales organization? Surprise, surprise! Mercedes tuning!

And so, in addition to individual conversion kits for Porsche, Jaguar, and VW, a complete spoiler program for the entire Daimler-Benz range was set up.

In this way, what was previously a trading company pure and simple has become a styling company as well.

Daimler-Benz AG

To the intense surprise of many, though not totally unexpected, the Stuttgart factory also profits from the styling and tuning market.

Following in the wake of the sixteen-valve cars, fitted with spoilers at the factory and based on the compact 190 series, the owners of less powerful versions without spoilers acquired since the end of 1985 can obtain the styling parts for the sixteen-valve model from the factory. The same applies to chassis modifications.

Duchatelet

This Belgian firm claims to offer "the cream of the cream." The company's original slogan is "Nothing great was ever born of compromise." The company has specialized in the field of tuning and styling Mercedes-Benz models since 1980 and is one of the most exclusive and reputed firms of its kind, providing elegant, conservative styling.

In addition to conventional add-on bodywork parts for all current Daimler-Benz limousine models, Duchatelet is particularly strong on interior styling, making full use of wood and leather. Chassis extensions, security armor plating, and recently wing doors for the S class are also obtainable from Duchatelet.

ES

This Bavarian company supplies motorcycle and automobile accessories. In addition to bodywork conversion kits for Audi and VW models, the company also supplies aerodynamic parts for the Mercedes 190 series.

Gemballa

Uwe Gemballa is one of the best known of all German car stylists and tuners. Since the foundation of the company at the end of the 1970's, it has specialized in the tuning and styling of Porsche models. For a relatively short time, Gemballa has also given the same treatment to Daimler-Benz products.

In the past, converted Mercedes models tended to look rather staid. So far as the exterior was concerned, the parts were mainly brought in from another manufacturer. This has now changed completely. Gemballa claims to build "the widest SEC coupe there is." It will be interesting to see what other ideas the company comes up with for Daimler-Benz, especially the new models in the top price category that in the future will come from the factory fully styled for sporting purposes. The Porsche show that they put on can expect stiff competition.

GFG

Things started up in 1981 at GFG with turbo technology for Daimler-Benz diesel cars. After that, the emphasis was on convertibles, long-wheelbase limousines, and armor-plated vehicles, based on the last middle-range series W 123 and the S class.

GFG has now tried its hand for the first time at a sports car design of its own based on the mechanical parts of the new Daimler-Benz middle-range W 124.

Haslbeck

The Haslbeck brothers started to build up their company, founded in 1979, with accessories for cross-country vehicles. Later, they added spoiler kits manufactured specifically for Japanese car manufacturers.

For the first time, the company is now offering its own program of cars, which are sold direct. The base model is the Daimler-Benz middle range W 124.

HF

HF began styling in 1979 with the VW Golf. Since 1981, it has specialized in Daimler-Benz models and now supplies a range of styling parts for all current Mercedes models.

Isdera

Behind the name Isdera (*Ingenieurburo fur Styling, Design und Racing*, which means Engineering Bureau for Styling, Design and Racing) is no less a person than Eberhard Schulz. It is Schulz's ambition to "reawaken motoring instincts that are becoming progressively stunted by the almost total uniformity of today's cars." He is achieving it with the aid of two striking short-run production sports cars, based mechanically on the Daimler-Benz. The prices for these breathtaking vehicles start at around 125,000 marks and finish up at levels that command respectful silence.

Kamei

KAMEI—the name is an abbreviation of the name of the founder, Karl Meier—is, together with BBS and Zender, the largest manufacturer of mass-produced parts in the spoiler business.

The company was founded in 1949 and grew up with a whole palette of automobile accessories, starting with flower vases and finishing with holders for beakers. Spoiler parts were added in the 1970's. The business really began to flourish when the company started offering add-on parts for the BMW and the VW (series 3 and the VW Golf).

Kamei then ventured into the preserve of Mercedes stylists with the S-class Mercedes and followed this with the 190 model.

Kodiak

The prototype Kodiak F1—the name smacks of the wide, wide world and the race track—was built in the vicinity of Stuttgart. Rather like its name, the body shell has some very exotic features.

The thoroughbred sports car, equipped with wing doors, is the only model produced by its creator, Mlado Mitrovic, and is available on request with a V-8 Daimler-Benz engine.

Koenig Specials

"There is no wish that cannot be fulfilled. Koenig designers and technicians will accept any challenge." So reads the Koenig philosophy, recorded in the company's literature.

Beyond any doubt whatever, every product that leaves the Koenig Specials factory is absolutely magnificent. Not one of the cars modified by Koenig Specials could be described as anything but spectacular. This applies in particular to the Daimler-Benz SL-series roadsters, SE/SEL limousines, and SEC coupes, which Koenig Specials has been converting since 1984.

Just like the Ferraris, which they have been modifying since 1978, they run on the widest tires available on the market, have the most eye-catching styling and are so wide that it would be merely academic to inquire whether they could manage anything wider. In the meantime, Koenig is even offering "red-hot" supercharged engines for four-cylinder sixteen-valve cars and the V-8 fireballs—good-lookers, with plenty of pep.

Following the general trend toward more restrained styling, Koenig Specials has also introduced standard-width versions of Daimler-Benz limousines into its program since 1986.

Kugok

Show styling with lots of glamour and glitter, glowing with gold: TV, bar, and tables, and heaven knows what else besides—the list of accessories for Kugok models makes fascinating reading on its own! Naturally, it's all for the S-class Daimler. But one can also model one's dream car on the old Mercedes 600, with a Pullman hood costing as much as a VW Polo.

L'Etoile

Under the name of L'Etoile (Star), the Belgian firm of Ronny Coach Building modifies S-class Daimler-Benz models with internal and external styling, and in some cases with massive wheelbase extensions.

Lorenz + Rankl

The firm of Lorenz + Rankl specializes in convertibles. The company has also had considerable success with body styling for other tuning companies and importers. In addition, there are the fantastic Lorenz creations, such as the Silver Falcon and a replica of the AC Cobra, both of them incorporating Mercedes mechanical systems.

Lorinser (Sportservice Lorinser)

Lorinser has been well-known as a Daimler-Benz agent since 1932. It was this close connection that led, as a result of suggestions put forward by customers toward the end of the 1960's, to the germination of an idea to carry out styling modifications on the most powerful Mercedes cars, the 6.3-liter and 6.9-liter models.

This program, which Lorinser emphasized—a typical advertising slogan read "Most people talk of styling; we offer perfection"—duly had its effect, so that, in a very short space of time, Lorinser was one of the most famous and successful Daimler-Benz styling houses. It still is.

From 1977 onward, the firm optimized every single Daimler-Benz car—even the lowly cross-country vehicle (G model) and the small delivery vans were not forgotten.

The aluminum wheels, their own design, are an optical treat in themselves.

Lorinser has, without a doubt, one of the largest (if not *the* largest) programs of body conversion parts of all Mercedes tuners and stylists.

Lotec

Hiding behind this name is the well-known sports car designer and racing driver Lotterschmid, several times Europa Cup and German Racing Champion in cars that he built himself.

The firm, which came into being in 1962, was given the name Lotec in 1974, and at the same time started tuning Porsches. Since 1984, it has been tuning Daimler-Benz models. The program of mechanical and styling parts now covers the entire range of Daimler-Benz limousines.

MAE

This company, run by Manuela Muller, is still relatively new to the styling and tuning scene.

The old and the new middle-range Mercedes cars W 123 and W 124, as well as the 190 series (W 201) models, are all modified with a style of their own. Conversion parts are now available from MAE for S-class models as well.

MTS

The firm of MTS was founded in 1981. It specializes in interior and exterior styling of Mercedes-Benz models. The focus models are the 190 series and the discontinued and new middle-range W 123 and W 124.

Oettinger

Oettinger, a graduate in engineering technology and the "pope" of all VW tuners, who has been active in the business since 1947, has also gone over to Mercedes tuning. Or, to be more precise, by ministering to the 190 model with its sixteen-valve engine, using all his old skills, he has coaxed more power out of it. Oettinger has left styling alone—so far, at least.

It will be interesting to see how the old master gets on in this strange territory.

Sbarro

Franco Sbarro is undoubtedly one of the truly great names in the world of styling and, so far as show styling is concerned, probably the greatest. He is not interested at all in mass—only in class. Opinions of him and his work are as extreme as his creations themselves. And his creations are without doubt the works of a master.

Sbarro's repertoire extends from the mini-Mercedes roadster for children of the 1930's (which is available, reproduced on a 1:1 scale, for the public highway) through two-door and four-door gullwing models based on the S-class Mercedes to the two-seater or four-seater super sports cars with an open-ended price and a Mercedes V-8 twin-turbo-engine.

Franco Sbarro can consider himself lucky to have a clientele who is not only willing to pay almost any price—even to the point of giving a blank check—but also utter and complete confidence in him and his art.

Depending on the customer's mentality, Sbarro will discuss the car in advance, down to the last detail, or he will be given a free hand and can—theoretically, at least—present his client with the finished article.

In most cases, however, the customer will not be able to keep away from the dream car for long and will want to see it several times during the creative stages, especially since such a one-off creation can take months, or even more than a year, in production before it is ready to take out on the road and deliver to its new owner.

Schulz

Erich Schulz, a passionate stylist and tuner, sees the main emphasis of his work in "visual enhancements and improvements under the hood."

Schulz's tuning has become particularly well-known through his convertible form of the compact Mercedes and through his installation of the 5.0-liter V-8 engine from the S class in the 190 series.

His coupe variant of the Mercedes 190 is so far unique. Similarly comprehensive work is also being carried out on the new middle-range W 124. In addition to the conventional spoiler and engine tuning programs for the S class, there are also open versions based on the SEL, as well as wheelbase extensions that include what is according to Schulz the longest S-class Mercedes currently available. It is, believe it or not, a full two meters longer than the original. As the magazine *Sport Auto* so neatly put it in 1985, "Superlonglong."

SKV

SKV Styling offers conversion of the Mercedes 190 into a convertible with fixed window frames; in other words, a sort of convertible-limousine (landaulet).

Taifun

Taifun-Automobiltechnik, a firm specializing in grilles for every conceivable type of car, has also now turned its attention to the Mercedes 190.

Trasco

Trasco International has been operating as an independent car dealer in Europe since 1971; it presented its own conversions for the first time in 1985. These are based on the SE, SEC, and SEL class series, which can be equipped with wing doors and also extended.

Turbo-Motors

This firm, specializing in turbochargers, concentrates on Mercedes gas and diesel engines. Turbo-Motors can improve the performance of almost any engine currently in use in Mercedes series cars by adding a supercharger.

Zender

Albert Zender started on a small scale in 1969, producing racing seats. A few years later, he took advantage of the spoiler boom, especially the types used on BMW's and the VW Golf. Since then, his program has become very comprehensive, now including conversions of Daimler-Benz models. In addition to conventional spoiler programs for the Mercedes 190 series (W 201), the old and new middle-range models W 123 and W 124, the S class (W 126), and the SL models (R 107), Zender Exklusivauto—as one of its departments, specializing in exclusive styling and eschewing mass production, is called—is concerned only with special conversions, including dual-purpose vehicles and wide versions based on Mercedes models.

Only very few people know that Zender has such a specialist department, since the firm is far better known as a volume manufacturer of styling parts.

ABC: Mercedes 190 (W 201), standard version with SEC hood . . .

. . . wide version.

Lotec: Mercedes 200-300 (W 124).

HF: Mercedes 200-300 (W 124) with SEC hood.

MTS: Mercedes 200-300 (W 124).

◆ HF: Mercedes 190 (W 201) with SEC hood.   ◆ MTS: Mercedes 190 (W 201).

Zender: Mercedes S-class (W 126) with SEC hood.

Gemballa: Mercedes SEC series (W 126), wide version.

bb Auto (Buchmann): Convertible based on Mercedes SEC model (W 126).

ABC: Mercedes 500 SEL (W 126).

Koenig Specials: Mercedes SEC series (W 126), wide version.

Lorinser: Mercedes SEC series (W 126) with Lorinser wheels.

Ronny Coach Building: Mercedes S-class (W 126) imperial sedan L'Etoile.

ABC: Mercedes 200-300 (W 124), standard version.

ABC: Interior of Mercedes 500 SEC, convertible model.

ABC: Mercedes 500 SEC (W 126), wide version.

Lotec: Mercedes 190 (W 201), wide version.

Sbarro: Challenge, with S-class technology and twin-turbo engine.

◀ *Isdera: 108i coupe with wing doors and S-class technology.*

Lorenz + Rankl: Silberfalke (Silver Falcon) with S-class technology.

◆ Zender: Mercedes SL series (R 107) with round headlamp grille and Zender wheels.

◆ Lorinser: Mercedes SL series (R 107).

Chapter 10

The oldies

Given the extent and importance of styling and tuning on the current Daimler-Benz models, it is scarcely imaginable just how little was done in the way of tuning and styling on their immediate predecessors, let alone on the series before that. The compact Mercedes 190 (W 201) has no predecessor; and virtually no styling or tuning was carried out on the SL series previous to the last one.

The first beginnings of engine tuning and bodywork modifications were seen on the large Mercedes models of the years 1968 to 1972, when the powerful 6.3-liter engine produced by AMG was first entered in touring car races. These machines appeared on the race track with extended fenders, but front spoilers, wings, and the like were still unheard of. The tiny "Fiat-Abarth racing hornets" had them when they left the factory, though, and after the small NSU TT and TTS models were equipped with these accessories as well, Daimler-Benz and the other marques soon took up the idea.

If a middle-range Mercedes W 107 or S-class models W 108 is to be mechanically modified or have its bodywork styled, it is advisable to turn to firms such as AMG or Lorinser, who can rightly be considered the pioneers of Daimler-Benz tuning and are in a position to offer an extremely comprehensive program. At the very least, they would be able to help one a step further.

There are a number of cheap products available, especially front spoilers for the old middle-range Mercedes W 107, that will not be discussed here. When considering engine and bodywork modifications on old models such as this one, one must ensure that TUV certificates are available. This will probably be the case only in rare instances.

The position is very much more promising for mechanical tuning and visual enhancements on the generation of models immediately prior to the current Daimler-Benz middle-range and S-class models. There are already reasonable numbers of conversions carried out on the W 123 and W 116 series for which TUV certificates have been issued.

AMG, Brabus, GFG, Lorinser, MAE, MTS, Schulz, Turbo-Motors, and Zender offer plenty of conversion variants on the middle-range W 123 models, from chassis kits through engine tuning to sets of spoilers, convertibles, and chassis extensions.

For the predecessor of the S class, the W 116, on the other hand, there are considerably fewer possibilities for engine and bodywork conversions. However, here again, AMG and Lorinser will be able to advise on the best course to take.

In addition, body styling parts can be obtained from the firm of UT. This company offers an inexpensive set of aerodynamic parts consisting of front spoiler, rocker panels, and rear apron, as well as an enormous rear wing for old S-class models.

In this respect, AMG confines itself to mechanical modifications, which consist of lowering the chassis and, in particular, tuning the engine.

Some of the modifications carried out on

🔼 *Lorinser: Old Mercedes S-class (W 116) with SEC hood.*

🔽 *D + W: Old Mercedes middle range (W 123) model.*

AMG: Old Mercedes T model (W 123).

the current S class W 126 can also be applied to the preceding W 116 models. As a very reputable manufacturer, AMG always points out the need for TUV certificates.

Lorinser offers styling parts for the old S-class models. It can even offer an SEC hood for the old W 116. In addition to the usual front spoiler/rocker panels/rear apron program, the company also supplies the typical Lorinser trunk lid with integral metal breakaway edge.

Neither trunk lid nor hood comes under the heading of "cheap products," but they will both cause the heart of a well-heeled W 116 fan to beat a little faster with nostalgia and affection.

A W 116 enhanced in this way, with such special parts and the Lorinser chassis, including 245/45 R 16 tires on nine-inch wheels, need not be hidden away from public view. Quite the reverse—such is its elegance that it will immediately attract astonished and envious glances.

The variety of tuning and styling parts offered for the recently discontinued W 123

models is already quite large. So far as improving engine performance is concerned, AMG offers a 2.8-liter power unit developing 155 kW (210 hp), which will improve the top speed of the limousine or coupe to over 130 mph and bring its acceleration from 0 to 60 mph down to under nine seconds. Chassis, exhaust unit, manual five-speed gearbox, an efficient braking system, and a limited slip differential are also available from AMG. Tires to suite this car go up to 225/50 R 16 on AMG 8×16-inch wheels.

As visual enhancements, AMG offers front spoiler, rocker panels, and rear apron, as well as a rear spoiler for the original trunk lid.

Brabus also offers a package similar to that available from AMG for the W 123.

The mechanical improvements possible consist of wheels and tires—up to 245/45 R 16 on 9×16 wheels—sports chassis, exhaust system, and performance tuning.

The additional performance obtained from the six-cylinder engine amounts to some 20 to 25

Brabus: Old Mercedes coupe (W 123) of the middle range.

hp (15 to 18 kW), and is achieved by conventional tuning without any need to increase engine capacity. The performance of four-cylinder power units can also be increased, but only on special request, as with the W 123 six-cylinder models.

With Brabus, the interior of the W 123—except for the usual things such as leather-covered steering wheel, wooden gearshift lever knob, and various additional instruments—can be embellished with genuine root wood. The cost of such enhancements, however, is only available on request.

The position is different, however, when it comes to the exterior. Front spoiler, rocker panels, and rear apron make up the standard program, as with the other firms. In addition, as with Lorinser, a trunk lid with integral breakaway edge is available to improve the airflow.

The firm of Brinkmeyer supplies a set of spoilers for the discontinued Daimler-Benz

middle-range models that differs considerably from that of its competitors. The angular front spoiler is carried through with fluted side panels on a level with the bumper, the fluting then being continued round the rear apron.

The giant accessories firm of D + W has also included the W 123 in its own homebred Daimler-Benz program and offers front spoiler, rear apron, and rocker panels. It even offers a freestanding rear wing for the discontinued middle-range Daimler-Benz models.

The emphasis in GFG's turbo and technology program is determined by quite different factors. The starting point for GFG's activities was turbo-engines for Daimler-Benz diesel cars, especially the W 123. The 240 D is thus available with a maximum output of 68 kW (92 hp), the 300 D with a maximum output of 84 kW (115 hp)—in the production models, it developed 65 kW (88 hp). Armor-plated vehicles for the middle-range Mercedes class are also available from GFG, and

Brinkmeyer: Old Mercedes middle-range (W 123) model.

as a speciality there is a two-door four-seater W 123 convertible. The convertible can be fitted on request with an electrohydraulic mechanism and has 225/50x15 tires fitted on 7x15 BBS wheels. The price of the package, as is usual in most such cases, is available on request.

Lorinser supplies more conventional body parts for the W 123, conveniently summarized in parts lists. Sportservice offers the W 123 owner wide tires up to 245/45 R 16 on 9Jx16 wheels and sports chassis, as well as steering wheels and seats for the interior, and has assembled a spoiler program for the exterior. There are front spoilers and rear aprons as add-on parts for the original bumpers, or as complete units integrated into the bumper in question; to add to this, one can have a matching set of rocker panels, an engine hood of the SEC type, the Lorinser trunk lid with breakaway edge, and a roof spoiler for the Model T.

As with other firms, the parts available from Lorinser for the W 123 are made from glass-fiber-reinforced plastic (GRP), a material that is not elastic, but nevertheless is tough and easy to repair.

MAE offers a speciality in W 123 styling: the Mercedes CE coupe is fitted with restrained fender extensions that suit this model extremely well. However, MAE also gives it a matching front spoiler, as well as a rear apron and very large tires, up to 285/40 R 15 on eleven-inch wheels on the rear axle. This necessitates lowering the chassis.

MTS's W 123 menu is rather more modest, and it only offers front spoiler, rocker panels, and rear apron. For many people, this is, in fact, quite enough.

In contrast to MTS, Schulz-Tuning also offers a trunk lid with breakaway edge and an engine hood with a wide grille, a la SEC coupe. The Mercedes Model T can also be enhanced to the same extent. The illustration shows a version with very harmonious fenders, the provision of which, it should be noted, involves expensive assembly and lacquering work. As a speciality, Schulz-Tuning offers, among others, extended-wheelbase models. The four-door or six-door imperial sedans can be "stretched" by up to two meters, and can be styled as well.

The activities of Turbo-Motors are chiefly

GFG: Convertible based on old W 123 series.

Lorinser: Old Mercedes Model T (W 123).

MAE: Old Mercedes W 123 in coupe style.

confined to engine tuning and, as the company's name suggests, to supercharging by means of turbochargers. Turbo-Motors stocks a performance-enhancing kit for the power units of the W 123 series, which will lift the 300 D (84 kW/115 hp instead of 64 kW/88 hp in the production model) as well as the 280E (161 kW/220 hp instead of the 136 kW/185 hp in the production model). In the case of the 240 D engine with an output of 48 kW/65 hp or 53 kW/72 hp in the production model, Turbo-Motors turbocharger pushes the output up to 60 kW/82 hp or 66 kW/90 hp. A special high-performance unit can actually help it to achieve 73 kW/100 hp, according to the manufacturer's claims. In the case of the 200 D variant, Turbo-Motors will not put a specific figure on the performance, but talks of a relative increase in performance of about twenty-five percent with the standard turbocharger and about forty-five percent with the high-performance turbocharger. Turbo-Motors will make all the necessary TÜV entries for a fee, which is certainly an advantage from the customer's point of view as well.

The firm of Zender is represented in every class of Daimler-Benz car, and its handiwork is thus to be found among the discontinued models as well. The Zender spoiler program for the W 123 must be among the most comprehensive of any tuning or styling company anywhere—and not without good reason. The parts represent relatively good value for money and blend in harmoniously with the overall appearance of the Mercedes bodywork due to their smooth surfaces. As with the parts supplied by Schulz-Tuning, they give the W 123 a tauter, more modern look, since the bodywork from the bumpers downward is more homogeneous and therefore more "conducive to better airflow," entirely in keeping with the present-day aerodynamically oriented generation of cars.

The variety of parts offered for the middle-range Mercedes cars that have just been discontinued is still so vast that there is surely something to suit all tastes, without having to make too many concessions. Engine modifications and interior styling are also possible, even if the variety of parts available is only a fraction of what is on offer for the current range of Daimler-Benz vehicles.

MTS: Old middle-range Mercedes (W 123).   Schulz: Old Mercedes Model T (W 123).

◆ Schulz: Imperial sedan version based on old Mercedes middle-range model (W 123).

◆ Zender: Old middle-range Mercedes (W 123) with Zender wheels.

Chapter 11

The Baby Benz

Whoever would have expected—until the compact Mercedes 190, known internally as the W 201, appeared on the scene—that a Daimler-Benz production model would present the styling fraternity with absolutely new prospects:

- The enhanced models catch the eye wherever they appear and contribute most decisively to the image of the production models.
- Mass and class are of equal importance.
- Everything that has so far been available only in very limited ranges, on the cheapest to the most luxurious cars, is available on the 190: styling at a cost ranging from 100 to 100,000 marks.

The range of styling possibilities is simply sensational, and nothing quite like it has ever been seen before. Whether styling or tuning is involved, it has become a sort of game—almost unlimited in its scope—that the styling artists play with the 190.

So far as the mechanical side is concerned, the range extends from the 190 diesel engine with turbocharger producing a modest 53 kW (72 hp) to the 5.0-liter V-8 engine producing 221 kW (300 hp), transplanted from the heavier S-class models to the relatively light bodywork of the 190. On the styling side, the range of possibilities extends from a simple set of round headlamps and a tiny rear wing to a super-wide model with massively extended fenders and chunky 285/40 wheels at the rear. There is even talk of huge 345/35 tires. And in this line of business, if

anyone even mentions something like that, sooner or later someone else will put it into effect.

It is particularly noticeable that since the introduction of the 190, the "metal bashers" have experienced an irresistible urge to set to work with their cutting tools in a way that has cost not only many a compact Mercedes 190 its "scalp." The rash of convertible models has reached epidemic proportions and even Skodas, minis, and Range-Rovers have not been spared, nor has the number or the appearance of the individual models made any difference: "Off with their heads!" has been the cry. It is therefore not surprising that there is already an amazing array of 190 convertibles available and that they take an astonishing variety of forms. Much the same can also be said of special conversions based on the compact Mercedes (which are the subject of a separate chapter).

It is true that at the time this book was written, there was no six-wheeled 190 to be found, no 190 imperial sedan, no 190 station wagon car, no gullwing version, nor has anyone built one with pop-up headlamps or a speedster variant. But who can tell what the conversion specialists will dream up next. As they have shown all too often in the past, they are quite capable of springing surprises on the market.

Only two factors could restrict these developments. First there is the new middle-range W 124, which as a larger and more expensive version of the 190 is currently preferred by the styling artists since it provides greater scope for expensive options than the smaller 190. Second, there is the recognition that sooner or later it will be impossible to reconcile the sensational effect produced, as expressed in terms of the enormous development costs involved, with common sense, as expressed in terms of profitability.

The sort of customer who is interested in such outlandish creations has always been rare, and is now rarer still. The worst part is when the cake has to be divided among an increasing number of companies, old and new. Competition can have the effect of prodding the market, but it can also result in bungling and botching.

The following sections are intended to give an overview of the various possibilities that exist for engine tuning and the tire, rim, and spoiler programs available. In the case of engine tuning, only the manufacturer's performance data are given, without any details of actual performance claimed; on the basis of the manufacturer's performance data, many of these claims are quite impossible to achieve. Anyone who is interested in such information should refer to the literature put out by the individual styling companies. The values quoted in this book are empirical and calculated values, based on objective tests carried out with identical or similar models.

Styling and mechanical enhancements

Styling covers every visible modification to the bodywork and the interior of a car. Convertibles, coupes, and special body shells are covered in a separate chapter. Nevertheless, conventional styling can be further subdivided into three distinct areas: styling modifications to the exterior bodywork, modifications to the interior, wheels.

Let us take a look at the wheels, that is, the combination of rims and tires.

As the variety is simply too vast, even for the expert, and is constantly changing anyway, a few words of advice are called for as to how best to proceed. There are three possible ways of

obtaining a reasonably reliable overview of the rims available for a certain model:

- study all the brochures put out by the manufacturers of rims or the catalogues produced by the major dealers in accessories
- "pick the brains" of the local tire or car dealer
- visit motor shows

If the first approach is taken, reading all the available catalogues and brochures, one cannot, of course, be sure of getting the overall picture. But it is a good way of getting a reasonable overview of what is available and of forming and testing one's own taste in such things, and one can then talk much more knowledgeably to dealers and exhibitors.

If the standard rims are to be changed for special rims, then it is advisable to order the car with steel rims and have them fitted with snow tires if one does not wish, for styling reasons, to afford oneself the luxury of a separate set of light-alloy rims and snow tires. The whole idea of changing over from normal tires to snow tires on the same light-alloy rims is rather senseless and puts considerable strain on both tires and rims. Apart from that, the tires must be carefully stored when not in use and the wheels must be balanced afresh after each change.

If snow tires are essential, then it is advisable either to accept some loss of visual appeal and drive on steel rims with snow tires, or to go the whole hog and invest in a complete set of light-alloy rims permanently fitted with high-grade snow tires, which are now available in quite considerable widths and for speeds up to 200 km/h or more. They can, of course, be correspondingly expensive.

So far as their appearance is concerned, special rims can be divided into three important groupings: lattice rims, spoke rims, aerodynamic rims.

The classic example of the lattice rim is the BBS rim. Its cross-spoke pattern is reminiscent of older classical spoke wheels. This type is now available from practically all manufacturers of rims, with the two sets of spokes running at various angles to one another. BBS also supplies one variant that reminds one visually of the extremely successful three-piece racing rim. The spoke rims with radiating spokes range from the classic Ferrari racing rims to the Alpina rims and, visually speaking, can be considered to be the successors of earlier coach wheels with only a few spokes. In this category, there are now two quite distinct variants produced by AMG and Lorinser for Daimler-Benz models. The AMG rims symbolize the sturdy solidity of racing wheels, while the Lorinser rims are rather in the nature of elegant three-piece rims with flat-surfaced spokes.

Finally, there are also the aerodynamic rims in the style of the sixteen-valve Daimler-Benz model, or the more flat-surfaced rims produced by AMG, Lorinser, Schulz, Zender, and so on, which are also frequently closely akin to the design of the original Daimler-Benz rims.

The range of tire and rim sizes available extends from the modest 195/60 on 6.5-inch or seven-inch rims through seven-inch and eight-inch rims with 205 and 225 tires. Up to these dimensions, it is relatively easy to accommodate the wheels in the fenders. In every case where rims of more than seven-inch width and tires larger than 205/50 are used, it is important to ensure that there is sufficient freedom of movement within the fenders when the suspension is in action and at full lock. It may be necessary for the wheelhousing to be flanged or all the fenders to be opened up a little more. With larger wheels than these, modifications to the wheelhousings will always be required. In extreme cases, with tire dimensions of 225/50 R 15 or 245/45 R 15 at the front and 285/40 R 15 or even 345/35 R 15 at the rear, the whole lot could only be accommodated in "chubby cheeks," that is, extended fenders. In such cases, the 190's waistline would be considerably increased, so that the car would measure almost two meters across—it would be extended by a good 10 cm on each side.

Such extreme wheel dimensions would, of course, automatically necessitate strengthening the chassis, with shock absorbers capable of withstanding the increased loads, and, if the largest combinations of tires and rims were used, with improved wheel suspension. In the less extreme cases, this could take the form of horizontally acting transverse control arm and shock absorber supports designed to prevent the sup-

port blocks on the bodywork from becoming bent, causing the shock absorbers to bend away. But there is also another possibility, the installation of a completely new suspension—taken, for example, from a larger model—that would be able to withstand the considerably increased loads without any problems. In any case, before making such a heavy investment and putting such large wheels on a car, one should also consider the fact that conversions of this sort can have considerable drawbacks despite the increased styling effect achieved.

One cannot afford to overlook the fact that comfort is always reduced by use of wide tires. The question therefore arises as to whether this is adequately compensated for by the increased road-holding it generally achieves. In addition, there is also the increased danger of hydroplaning to be considered; the contact pressure of the tires on the road surface drops sharply as the tire width increases, and this pressure is a decisive factor where hydroplaning is concerned. It is entirely possible for a car with wide wheels to get into difficulties at speeds as low as 50 mph in relatively light rain. This is a factor that should be taken very seriously when changing over to such wide tires.

A further drawback is the reduction in top speed and the greater weight of the wide wheels. In a production model of the 190 E, for example, the top speed is reduced by 10 to 12 km/h if 205 and 225 tires are mounted on the front and rear wheels and by 20 to 25 km/h if 225/50 tires are mounted at the front and 285/40 at the rear. This sizable difference is due to the higher wind resistance resulting from the increased cross section of the vehicle brought about by the increased tire sizes and extended fenders. In such cases, the only choice is between two alternatives: styling for show, regardless of the drop in top speed, which is something for the showoff rider perhaps, or "breathing" on the engine to give it a few more horsepower to compensate for the loss of power and to spare the driver the ignominy of being overtaken by every standard Golf GTI on the road.

The susceptibility to longitudinal grooves in the road surface, such as the central join in

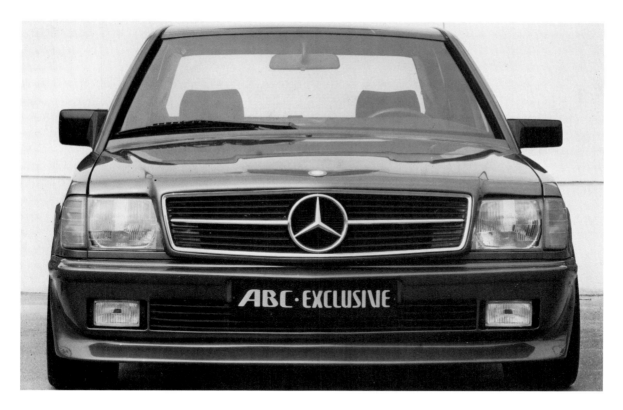

◆ ABC: Mercedes 190 (W 201) standard-width model with SEC-style hood.

◆ ABC: Mercedes 190 (W 201), wide version.

highways, and the straight-line characteristics suffer considerably in cars equipped with extremely wide tires since the carefully computed suspension geometry is completely overthrown and the car is more inclined to follow every irregularity in the road surface.

The effects of grooves, corrugations, loose stones, potholes, and other such irregularities are scarcely felt in today's production models, due to the arrangement of the suspension elements. In many cars running on wide tires, however, one feels as if one has been taken back to the bad old days when the driver constantly had to work hard at the steering wheel in order to compensate for the effects transmitted from the road through the steering. The overall result for the driver is an extremely tiring zig-zag line when driving at speed, especially on the highway, instead of driving along in a straight line in a relaxed manner. Anyone contemplating the purchase of a car with such wide tires would therefore be well advised to insist on a trial run first, preferably with a customer vehicle that has not been specially "trimmed." It certainly would not do any harm to have a chat with the owner of such a car about past experiences with it. Otherwise, the purchase could be deeply regretted for a long time to come and prove very expensive.

ABC

If we begin with this examination of the individual styling programs in alphabetical order, the first firm we encounter is ABC, based in Bonn. This styling company offers a whole range of conversions for the showoffs among the drivers of compact Mercedes.

ABC commences with a quite modest program for the standard-width models comprising front spoiler fenders, rocker panels, and rear apron fenders. A hood in GRP in the SEC coupe style can be added on request, and likewise in GRP, a trunk lid with a pronounced breakaway edge. This styling set is elegant and restrained, though the trunk lid adds a certain dash to the overall effect. If anyone prefers a wing, a freestanding rear spoiler can be supplied instead.

This tasteful exterior is complemented by a comprehensive range of interior features, from exclusive audio equipment, wood and leather trim, bar, and so on to video equipment.

For those customers whose taste is more daring, there is the ABC wide version of the Mercedes 190 (W 201). However, even this is relatively restrained, except perhaps for the rather pronounced "hips" above the rear wheels, forming the starting point for the wing mounted on the trunk top. However, the kit can be purchased without this. Further ABC specialities are designed for the set of convertibles (for details see Convertibles Based on the Mercedes 190).

Air Press

Air Press, so far known for their chromium-plated racking used for exhibition ramps, has now ventured into the world of enhancement and tried its hand on the Mercedes 190. In addition to an inexpensive package consisting of front spoilers, rocker panels, and rear apron, there is also the obligatory hood in the SEC style and a new trunk lid swept slightly upward, with grooving along the side, which merges into the rear roof pillars.

AMG

AMG, the pioneers of styling on the Daimler-Benz, has naturally taken a great deal of interest in the compact Mercedes. The result of all this is probably the most comprehensive range of styling and mechanical modifications of all. However, AMG does not set much store by convertibles and turbochargers—at least, not at the present time nor in the foreseeable future. This could change if Daimler-Benz were to install turbochargers ex-works and to find a serious partner with whom they could work on a convertible. For the time being, however, there is no work in this direction.

The AMG styling program starts with the standard-width model and offers a set consisting of front spoiler, rocker panels, and rear apron,

Air Press: Mercedes 190 (W 201) with SEC-style hood.

with an optional spoiler lip made out of plastic material molded onto the trunk lid or a free-standing wing on the lid.

The wider version of the AMG conversion kit for the 190 is rather restrained in style, despite an increase in the width of the car at fender height. The front fenders are entirely of GRP; the rear ones have so far also been made of GRP and were intended for sticking onto the original fenders, but are now being manufactured of pressed steel in one piece, which has greatly reduced manufacturing problems and led to a considerable improvement in quality.

Up to now, metal parts have been used by styling companies only for expensive one-off items, since they either had to be fabricated by hand, which was time-consuming and costly, or called for very expensive presses. Nevertheless, the tooling costs for the very flat and relatively small rear extended fenders are still within acceptable limits. On the other hand, spoilers,

rocker panels, and hoods of pressed steel are out of the question for styling firms on grounds of cost. The price of the machine tools required for each part is half a million to a million marks, and often higher than that—quite apart from the fact that one has still to find a manufacturer with the right kind of presses to take the tools.

AMG also has a wide range of features for the interior of the 190. Practically everything is available, from top-quality wood to complete leather trim.

AMG also offers a wide range of features for the engine apart from turbochargers. The tuning of diesel engines has been removed from the program again, however, whereas the tuning of gas engines starts with the 2.0-liter engine for the 190: 106 kW (145 hp) at 5750 rpm and 192 Nm at 4500 rpm are the salient points, good enough to produce a figure of less than ten seconds for 0 to 60 and a top speed of just on 130 mph.

A more powerful, but also more expensive,

AMG: Mercedes 190 (W 201), standard version with AMG rims.

solution for the 2.0-liter variant has been found by increasing the capacity to 2.3 liters. This produces 117 kW (160 hp), also at 5750 rpm, and 215 Nm at 4750 rpm. This accelerates the compact Mercedes from 0 to 60 in under nine seconds and gives it a top speed of 133 mph.

On the sixteen-valve model, potential output at an unchanged capacity of 2.3 liters is 151 kW (205 hp) at 6500 rpm and 251 Nm at 4500 rpm. This gives it an acceleration from 0 to 60 of under 7.5 seconds and a top speed of 150 mph.

As top of the range, where engines are concerned, AMG has installed in the compact Mercedes 190 the new 3.2-liter six-cylinder engine, which is an enlarged version of the engine from the 300 E middle-range model. This engine produces 180 kW (245 hp) and maximum torque is 324 Nm. This performance propels it from 0 to 60 in less than seven seconds and gives it a top speed of 155 mph.

As can be seen, AMG is not much given to experimentation where engines are concerned, preferring to rely on what is already well tried and tested. Hans-Werner Aufrecht, the head of the firm, underlies this philosophy, since most of his customers clock up a considerable annual mileage and are less concerned with maximum performance. However, should anyone express that kind of interest, AMG has something up its sleeve in the shape of a V-8 engine with four valves per cylinder and bags of output. These engines are, however, available only on the middle-range W 124 models and upwards at appropriate prices. Top-flight technology naturally goes hand in hand with top prices.

BBS

Anyone who is interested in enhancing a 190 with aerodynamic parts produced by BBS, the well-known manufacturer of rims, will be

◆ *AMG: Mercedes 190 (W 201), wide version.*   ◆ *AMG: Interior.*

BBS: Mercedes 190 (W 201) with BBS rims.

pleasantly surprised to find that prices for them are not outlandish. The carefully assorted and balanced program of styling parts is complemented by the well-known one-piece and three-piece BBS lattice rims and the BBS chassis. The bodywork set consists of a front spoiler in the typical BBS grooved design, modest rocker panels, and a rear apron. The overall impression is rounded off by a spoiler lip mounted on the original trunk lid.

Brabus

The Brabus program for 190 conversions is considerably more comprehensive. In addition to several bodywork variants, the company offers a wide range of features to improve performance and enhance the interior. Brabus supplies front spoilers, rocker panels, and rear aprons to modify the exterior of the 190. A trunk lid with breakaway edge and a hood in the SEC style are available on request. There is also an

independent front spoiler for the sixteen-valve model.

Brabus has a wide range of engine modifications available with different performance levels. These start with conventional mechanical aids to improve performance on the 2.0-liter engine and extend right up to V-8 engines that have been taken from the S class models and installed in the compact Mercedes. The 2.0-liter variant is said to produce 110 kW (150 hp) at 5500 rpm, with a maximum torque of 195 Nm at 4700 rpm. That is enough to give it a top speed of 130 mph, with acceleration from 0 to 60 in about nine seconds. If the 2.0-liter unit is also fitted with a turbocharger, then an output of 132 kW (180 hp) is reached at 5300 rpm and the maximum torque is increased to 235 Nm at 3450 rpm. These figures should suffice for acceleration from 0 to 60 in less than eight seconds and a top speed of approximately 142 mph.

The Brabus 190 with a V-8 S class engine appears rather bulky. The two variants available—

Brabus: Mercedes 190 (W 201).

one completely standard, the other slightly tuned—produce 170 kW (231 hp) and 184 kW (250 hp) respectively at 4750 rpm, each with a maximum torque of 405 Nm at 3000 rpm. The promise of performance in excess, and with all the nonchalance of the V-8 engine, is an extremely attractive prospect. But here again there is a drawback. The heavy engine makes the compact Mercedes 190 front-heavy.

Naturally, conversions on this scale do not come cheaply if the job is done properly. One has only to think of the cost of the power unit alone. Then there are very extensive modifications to the chassis, the understructure, and the transmission. All of this has a price. Potential customers should ask what it will be, specifying their product requirements, for again it is a question of "details available on request."

Car Design Schacht

Car Design Schacht is a styling company based in Munich that also specializes in styling on Mercedes models. Apart from a program of rather solid-looking bodywork parts—front spoilers, rocker panels, rear aprons, SEC-style hoods—the company also offers wood paneling and special equipment for the interior. If requested, they can also provide chassis and engines with enhanced performance.

Carlsson Motortuning

The firm of Carlsson has a special background. The Swedish rally driver Ingvar Carlsson has gone into business—believe it or not—with one of the former BMW tuning aces, Andreas Hartge. The latter's experience has borne visible fruits in their first joint project and the results are immediately available in three ways: the Carlsson rims, which are almost identical with those Hartge produced for BMW; the sophisticated styling of the bodywork set; and a 2.0-liter engine increased to 2.4 liters.

Car Design Schacht: Mercedes 190 (W 201).

The spoiler set is very smooth-surfaced and restrained in style. This is particularly noticeable in the wide version with extended fenders; these are extremely elegant, being concentrated around the wheel cut-out and giving the 190 a very dynamic appearance, especially when a hood closely akin to that of the SEC coupe is also added.

To quote Carlsson himself, however, the emphasis is on engine tuning. It is Carlsson's intention to bring his very considerable racing experience to bear on the development of chassis and engines. The results are already plain to see in the form of a 2.4-liter engine, with plenty of pulling power, which produces 126 kW (180 hp) at 6000 rpm and achieves its maximum torque of 228 Nm at 4000 rpm. The top speed of this modified 190 is 136 mph, and it will accelerate from 0 to 60 in a little under eight seconds.

Even greater performance is provided by the V-8 power unit taken from the S-class model and installed in the compact 190, either in stan-dard form or with performance still further enhanced. The specially tuned V-8 engine, producing 200 kW (272 hp) at 5650 rpm and maximum torque of 420 Nm at 3100 rpm, in particular, promises performance in abundance. A top speed of 155 mph and 0 to 60 in a little over six seconds can certainly be achieved. The problem here, as with other V-8 engine transplants, is that the compact Mercedes becomes front-heavy due to the massively heavy V-8 engine block.

This is not a problem that Carlsson Motor-tuning's introductory model has to contend with. Its straightforward 2.0-liter power unit produces 109 kW (148 hp) at 6000 rpm and achieves its maximum torque of 188 Nm at 4600 rpm. Even with this engine, which requires only a relatively modest capital investment on the part of the customer, the car can be relied on to provide some highly enjoyable driving. A figure of less than ten seconds for acceleration from 0 to 60 and a top speed of just over 130 mph can be confidently expected.

Carlsson: Mercedes 190 (W 201) with Carlsson rims.

D + W

D + W, the largest dealer in accessories in the Federal Republic (West Germany), has drawn up its own independent styling program for the compact Mercedes, in which it gives particular attention to the styling of both bodywork and interior. There are several bodywork styling sets for the 190. The firm supplies all parts, such as front spoilers, rocker panels, rear aprons, and rear spoilers, in a number of different variants. A radiator grille with broad cross struts of GRP can be supplied on request, and the original broad-beam headlamps can be replaced with twin cir-

cular headlamps. This is an alternative to the combination of rectangular headlamps and SEC-type grille for those who prefer it. It is bound to attract attention, since who would expect a Mercedes of the current series to appear with twin circular headlamps!

As part of its Mercedes program, D + W offers its own rims, which have a relatively smooth surface.

Whatever is good for the stylist is hardly likely to do Daimler-Benz much harm. No sooner said than done—and the styling set for the sixteen-valve 190 model was developed.

109

D + W: Mercedes 190 (W 201) styling set II.

This set of plastic styling parts can now be obtained through the Daimler-Benz dealer organization of the entire compact Mercedes series. As a result, any 190 diesel, for example, can be dressed up on the outside like a sixteen-valve model.

The visual attraction and the independence of the Mercedes 190 E 2.3-16 are, of course, undermined in this way. The question is now: Is this balanced out by the additional business the plastic parts bring in? Whatever the results of that deliberation may be, the almost classical and much discussed body styling parts, with their smooth surfaces and prominent wing, can now be attached to any 190 model without any problems. The fact that they have given rise to so much discussion is in itself a good sign; there can certainly be no doubt that the design is restrained, with clean lines, and technically well-founded, and it is equally clear that the wing has achieved a wide measure of acceptability as a result of this design.

If a stylist had created this styling set, then it would probably have been dismissed as "reserved to the point of boring." Since the manufacturers themselves have put it on the market, it will perhaps be judged by many to be "striking to the point of obtrusive"—on which one could no doubt construct a whole new theory of relativity with regard to taste!

Duchatelet

Among the styling programs offered, that put forward by the Belgian styling firm of Duchatelet would certainly fall into the category of "unobtrusive." This company offers two variants for the compact Mercedes, one with extended fenders and one without. They differ considerably in style, though. The standard version looks quite ingenuous and well-behaved, whereas the wide version with its add-on wheelhouse exten-

110

Duchatelet: Mercedes 190 (W 201).

Duchatelet: Interior.

Daimler-Benz: Mercedes 190 E 2.3-16 (W 201).

sions and the pronounced, deep edges that run from the front spoiler via the rocker panels to merge with the rear apron give the 190 an appearance of great power. An extremely elegant, flat freestanding wing complements the spoiler package. Duchatelet also approaches the interior of the 190 in the same restrained manner. Finest quality materials, such as wood, velour, and leather, are combined in a restrained and classical style to achieve an attractive overall effect. The designers in charge of Duchatelet clearly attach little or no importance to trivia and technical "toys" in the interior, to say nothing of gimmicks.

ES

The Lower Bavarian firm of ES fitted the compact Mercedes out in a massive custom-built styling "suit." It is not exactly intended for people of retiring disposition who do not wish to attract attention to themselves. The huge freestanding rear wing alone is enough to attract the attention of anyone within sight, and reminds one—depending on one's attitude toward such things—of the race track or teenage extravagance. The style of the smooth-surfaced parts themselves, with their clean lines, is somewhat reminiscent of the factory-supplied sixteen-valve styling set, but the pronounced lips on the front spoiler and rear apron provide more than a little sporting flavor for the eye. The subconscious impression, resulting from the clearly defined outlines, parting edges, ventilation and jacking points, and a narrow opening through which the end of the exhaust pipe protrudes, is one of technical functionality.

The styling parts produced by the firm of HF are the opposite of those produced by ES. The visual impact of the HF parts is concentrated in essence on the grooving that runs from the front

HF: Mercedes 190 (W 201) with SEC-style hood.

spoiler across the panels applied to the doors. The overall impression is completed by a rear apron and, optionally, an SEC-style hood.

Kamei

The well-known volume manufacturer Kamei also offers a spoiler set, known as X1, for the W 201. It consists of front spoiler, rocker panels, rear apron, and a rubber spoiler mounted on the trunk lid.

Lorinser

The firm of Lorinser offers one of the most comprehensive programs of styling parts for all 190 models. The illustrations show the standard and the wide versions, selected from a wide variety of different models. Between these two are a number of other variants that have certain visual similarities to the two models shown. For example, the firm supplies front spoilers for attaching either below the original front apron or in one piece integral with the front apron. The same applies to the rear apron, which can be supplied as a part designed for screwing below the original apron or as a complete rear apron/bumper.

The rocker panels are also adapted to match the particular fender variant used. They are lengthened to a greater or lesser extent depending on whether the fenders or wheelhouses are extended or not. There is also a new Lorinser SEC-style bonnet, though this is of only approximately the same width as the original grille on the 190, so that the original fog lamps are not masked in the same way as they are with the wide SEC hood variants. Nevertheless, a considerable part of the effect of width created by the SEC hood is lost in the process. Naturally, the view-

Kamei: Mercedes 190 (W 201).

er's subjective feelings play a decisive part in deciding whether the combination of the wide SEC-style hood and the relatively narrow compact Mercedes has been successful or not.

Lorinser trunk lid is one of its particular specialities. The company made this styling feature popular in the first place and started a boom in trunk lid enhancements. In the meantime, apart from the simple Lorinser breakaway edge, there are quite a number of variants of different heights and widths, which either extend into the region of the fender or are entirely restricted to the trunk lid. In the end it comes down to a question of cost, since mounting the lips involves a considerable amount of welding or soldering, filling, and lacquering.

Lorinser also has a lot of quality features to offer for the interior of the compact Mercedes: wood, leather, audio and video equipment, bar, telephone, and the like—and if anyone should want it, the Mercedes 190 can be lowered as well.

The company also has the best interests of its customers at heart in offering its Airclean System, a filter system that cleans the incoming air at times when it contains an unusually high proportion of noxious substances, such as in traffic jams, at traffic lights, and in tunnels.

Lotec

The firm of Lotec, which belongs to the racing driver Lotterschmid, also offers a standard version and a more expensive wide version of the Mercedes 190. In the case of the standard version, the styling consists of a front spoiler, rocker panels, and rear apron in a very restrained style. As options, one can order a new hood either in the SEC style or—and this is the peculiarity—in a more smooth-surfaced form, reminiscent of the original hood. By way of contrast to the standard model, the Lotec radiator grille is fully integrated into the hood, giving it a

114

Lorinser: Mercedes 190 (W 201) standard version.

smooth, more modern look, while still retaining the original appearance of the 190.

In the Lotec wide version, which is primarily intended as a vehicle for the sixteen-valve engine, the visual impression is dominated by the fender extensions, which blend into the rocker panels without any transition or seam. The wheelhouses, which are extended outwards, enable tires of the order of 245/45 VR 16 on nine-inch rims to be accommodated. The whole ensemble gives a sporty impression, enhanced by the level of performance.

Let us first start with the lower-powered versions: Daimler's small diesel models all get equipped with turbochargers, the 2.0-liter diesel producing 66 kW (90 hp) at 4500 rpm and the 2.5-liter diesel producing 84 kW (115 hp) at 4500 rpm. For the export market, these figures are increased by 7 kW (10 hp).

In the case of gas engines, a turbo variant is available for the 2.0-liter engine, producing 132 kW (180 hp) at 5100 rpm. This is sufficient to ensure extremely good performance, of the same order as that of the factory-supplied sixteen-valve engine, 0 to 60 in less than eight seconds and a top speed of 139 to 142 mph.

In addition to that, there is another variant of the 2.0-liter engine that has been enlarged to 2.3-liter and develops 110 kW (149 hp), which is good for acceleration from 0 to 60 in less than ten seconds and a top speed of 130 mph.

Top of the range from Lotec is a 2.3-liter sixteen-valve engine with turbocharger and a claimed output of 220 kW (300 hp) at 6000 rpm and powerful torque of 380 Nm at 4500 rpm. This engine is claimed to have thirty percent more output than the normally aspirated factory engine at as low as 2000 rpm. The reason for this is the compression ratio of 9:1, which is enormous for a turbo-engine. According to the manufacturer, this is made possible by a freely programmable form of ignition with microprocessor control, which constantly monitors actual measurement data on engine loads by means of

Lorinser: Mercedes 190 (W 201) wide version.

measuring transducers and uses these to determine the amount of fuel to be injected and the moment of ignition for each individual cylinder. If these data were actually achieved, the car would have to be capable of 0 to 60 in under six seconds and a top speed of over 161 mph, the sort of performance obtainable with the massive V-8 engines of the S-class models, but without the drawback of the extra weight on the front axle.

As everything about the operation of the 2.3-liter sixteen-valve turbo-engine is incomparably more hectic than with the 5.0-liter or 5.6-liter V-8 engine, just from the point of view of the noise level alone, there are bound to be differences of opinion about the alternative.

Both of them have performance in abundance—perhaps too much for cars of this size in normal road traffic, since this sort of power requires a considerable degree of self-discipline coupled with considerable driving skill. An inexperienced driver, who might easily be pro-

voked by the sight of a Ferrari, Porsche, or some other high-performance car disappearing into the middle distance, would very quickly overstep the limits of his own skill, find himself running out of road, and need a goodly portion of luck to escape any serious consequences.

MAE

MAE, managed by Manuela Muller, is based in Stuttgart, the home of Mercedes-Benz, and has developed its own individual style to make the 190 look more powerful—wide and low. To start with, they have given it hefty wheels (225/45 VR 16 on nine-inch rims at the front and 245/45 VR 16 on eleven-inch rims at the rear). The fenders have of course had to be extended to accommodate these huge wheels. MAE has a special approach to this problem: Starting from the original waistline, the side sections extend outward uniformly and at a relatively sharp angle

116

Lotec: Mercedes 190 (W 201) wide version.

until they reach the upper edge of the fenders. Then there is a small shoulder as well. The car appears to bulge in a quite unusual way, quite different from the type of "snowplow and guttering" styling employed with front spoilers and rocker panels.

The front spoiler and rear apron are still largely in keeping with the original parts, but are extended outward as well, due to the extended fenders. The rocker panels are not noticeable as such since they join with the side panels and the door sill roundly and smoothly, just like the originals. In spite of that, the effect achieved is of a wasp-waist, very pleasing to the eye, with wider bodywork on a level with the axles and narrower original bodywork on a level with the doors.

The harmonious ensemble is complemented by an unobtrusive hood in the style of the original, but flatter and wider, so that the impression obtained from a front view is more that of an S-class model.

The only feature that is very obtrusive, and takes some getting used to, is the roof spoiler mounted freestanding on the roof immediately above the rear window. Apart from the doubtful benefit of such a part and the problems it poses in terms of visual impact, there is the whole question of the advisability of drilling in the roof the number of holes required to mount it, which must call for considerable enthusiasm. If the car were to be sold again at a later date, and a potential buyer did not like the roof spoiler, then it would be too late to carry out any repairs except perhaps at a cost out of all proportion to the cost and usefulness of the roof spoiler.

But leaving that feature aside, the MAE 190 is very successful all round, with a look that is quite different from all other enhanced or converted 190's. However, the conversion work, which up to now has always been carried out by MAE itself, comes with a considerable price tag. Anyone interested should contact the firm about prices, since, once again, it is a matter of "details available on request."

MAE: Mercedes 190 (W 201) wide version with roof spoiler.

MTS

The bodywork styling parts produced by the firm of MTS, which is also based in the Stuttgart area, are clearly defined and normal in appearance and price. The MTS styling set, which has a number of crafty features, consists of front spoiler, rocker panels, and rear apron. There are also fender extensions to go with the rocker panels, and these are mounted on the mudguards, as well as a rear spoiler, which is molded to fit the trunk lid.

As with almost all other Daimler-Benz styling firms, MTS will also lower the chassis and supply a different set of wheels.

Koenig Specials

Koenig Specials in Munich and the old-established Tuning Werkstatt of the VW specialist Oettinger carry out engine tuning only on the 190—so far, at any rate.

Whereas Oettinger follows his successful principle of stepping up performance by increasing the engine capacity, Koenig Specials achieves its end by means of a turbocharger. Oettinger offers two variants: one a twin-valve 2.0-liter engine increased to 2.3 liters and producing 106 kW (145 hp) at 5000 rpm, with a maximum torque of 215 Nm at 3500 rpm; and the other a 2.3-liter four-valve engine increased to 2.6, producing 155 kW (211 hp) at 5700 rpm with a maximum torque of 286 Nm at 4300 rpm. The two-valve car has a top speed of just on 130 mph and accelerates from 0 to 60 in less than ten seconds, while the four-valve version can manage 0 to 60 in about seven seconds and reaches a top speed of 148 mph.

Koenig Specials increase the performance of the sixteen-valve engine by adding a turbocharger, the best version producing 191 kW (161 mph). This should mean a time of fractionally more than six seconds for 0 to 60. The top speed is said to be 155 mph.

Schulz: Mercedes 190 (W 201).

Schulz

The firm of Schulz, based in the vicinity of Monchengladbach, was one of the forerunners of the more extreme types of engine tuning and styling. The boss of the firm, Erich Schulz, was the first to take a five-liter V-8 engine from an S-class model and install it in a compact Mercedes 190. He was also the first person to build a convertible based on the 190, and he is still the only one to build a 190 coupe.

Where styling is concerned, Schulz was more inclined to be conventional. All his cars were low-slung, wide, well rounded, and suitably eye-catching. The 190 lends itself well to this sort of treatment.

Schulz builds 190's with and without extended fenders, the latter being far more complicated and expensive since the extension has to be riveted to the bodywork and the transition seam filled in. After that, a complete respray is necessary, up to the waistline at least.

So far as the engine is concerned, Erich

Schulz decided from the very beginning on a "heart transplant." The engines transplanted in this case are the six-cylinder or eight-cylinder engines normally used in S-class models. The lowest level of performance offered is that of the six-cylinder series engine of 2.8-liter capacity, which produces 136 kW (185 hp) at 5800 rpm. The maximum torque of 240 Nm is developed at 4500 rpm. An acceleration from 0 to 60 in about 7.5 seconds can be expected, and a top speed of just on 142 mph.

The medium level of performance is provided by the V-8 engine from the 380 SE, which produces 150 kW (204 hp) at 5250 rpm and maximum torque of 315 Nm at only 3250 rpm. This should easily suffice for a top speed of 145 mph, and 0 to 60 in less than seven seconds. Thrown in for nothing is the gratifying purring of the V-8 engine and the powerful traction of the massive engine mounted over the front axle.

The crowning glory of the series is the use of the 5.0-liter V-8 engine in its standard produc-

Vestatec: Mercedes 190 (W 201) with SEC hood.

tion form. Schulz showed the way with this engine, which develops 170 kW (231 hp) at 4750 rpm and maximum torque of 405 Nm at 3000 rpm. A chariot like this reaches 60 mph from a standing start in less than seven seconds and can achieve a top speed of a good 148 mph.

Taifun

Taifun is the best known manufacturer of special radiator grilles, making his name in particular with the twin rectangular headlamp grille borrowed from the Audi Quattro for the old BMW 3-series models. On the 190, Taifun uses twin circular headlamps instead of the original wide-beam headlamps, and a smooth-surfaced radiator screen in place of the Mercedes chromium grille.

Turbo-Motors

Turbo-Motors, as their name indicates, use turbochargers for supercharging. Their wide-ranging program extends from the smallest diesel engine of 2.0-liter capacity through small gas engines that develop 118 kW (160 hp) and 132 kW (180 hp) respectively from a 2.0-liter capacity to finish with the S-class twin-turbo developing 220 kW (300 hp).

Vestatec

The firm of Vestatec produces quite a number of spoiler sets for Japanese and German cars. It was therefore impossible for this manufacturer to bypass the Mercedes 190. It now offers two variants: One is conventional and consists of a front spoiler, rocker panels, and a rear apron—there is also a Vestatec radiator

Zender: Mercedes 190 (W 201) standard version.

screen and a freestanding rear wing; the second variant was on the market earlier and is characterized by a striking grooved design that extends from the front spoil via door panels to the rear apron. This is complemented by extended fenders and a rear spoiler mounted on the original trunk lid.

Zender

The well-known Zender program offers a variety of spoilers for the 190. There are no fewer than three completely different sets available for the compact Mercedes. The program starts with the standard version of the 190. The set consists of front spoiler and rear apron, screwed on below the original bumpers, and complemented by a set of rocker panels. The corresponding rear wing, however, is not at all restrained in style and extends along the rear fenders almost as far as the rear roof pillars.

Zender's second level of styling consists of front spoiler and rear apron/bumper, together with wide rocker panels that merge into beautifully curved fender extensions. The whole ensemble can be combined with Zender's own matching rims.

Zender's wide version is very wide, with "stretched" mudguard extensions instead of simple extended fenders. This is responsible for the powerful and massive impression that this version creates.

Overview

The styling programs of the various companies shows a variety of possibilities such as has

◆ *Zender: Mercedes 190 (W 201) with extended fenders.* ◆ *Zender: Mercedes 190 (W 201) wide version.*

ABC: Convertible based on the Mercedes 190 (W 201), with spoilers and rims.

never before been available. With no other car before has there ever been such a range of tuning and styling options as with the compact Mercedes.

From the restrained to the extremely conspicuous, the elegant to the massive, the conservative to the progressive—every nuance is represented in the styling features offered. It is very hard to imagine that one could not find something to suit everyone's taste in all the spoiler programs.

There are also virtually no limits to the possibilities for enhancement of the interiors, except perhaps those imposed by financial constraints.

The same applies to engine tuning and chassis enhancements. Tires of the order of 195/50 VR 15 on 6.5-inch rims up to 345/35 VR 15 on thirteen-inch rims are an expression of unbridled enthusiasm where the chassis is concerned, in some cases to the point of losing all reasonable

self-control. This also applies to the engine: 2.0-liter diesel turbo-engines of 66 kW (90 hp) are the lower limit, while 2.3-liter sixteen-valve turbo-engines of 220 kW (300 hp) and 5.0-liter V-8 engines souped up to 200 kW (272 hp) from the S-class models are the upper limit. However, there is little doubt that some companies will not shrink from installing the new 5.6-liter V8 engine with its 200 kW (272 hp) in standard form in the compact Mercedes.

If one adds four valve heads à la AMG, one or two turbochargers, or a mechanical compressor to the 5.6-liter power unit, then 294 kW (400 hp) would be there almost for the asking. What would happen to the 190 then is extremely difficult to say. On a purely theoretical basis, such a car would be capable of speeds just about on the sound barrier of 186 mph, and if the aerodynamics were refined a little by adding, say, a factory spoiler set, it could even break it.

ABC: Convertible based on the Mercedes 190 (W 201), wide version with SEC-style hood.

At a stroke, the Baby Benz would challenge the position of such super sports cars as the Ferrari GTO, the Lamborghini Countach Quattro Valvole, and the Porsche 959. Isn't that crazy? Crazy, yes—but also realistic!

Convertibles

In addition to attaching bodywork parts such as front spoilers, rocker panels, modified hood, rear wings, and so on, styling firms have also converted the production model of the 190 into a convertible, in exactly the same way as with the S-class models.

ABC

The most comprenhensive convertible program is that of ABC, which offers a two-seater two-door roadster, a four-seater two-door convertible, and a four-seater four-door variant. The two-door convertible is further available in a wide version with tires of the order of 285/40 at the rear. All these open-air models are available with ABC's own spoiler parts. Even ABC's SEC-style hood and the trunk lid with breakaway edge are available on request. ABC offers these 190-based convertibles with either manual or electro-hydraulic operation of the top—the latter at a considerable extra cost, of course. When down, the top is hidden away beneath a leather or a hard cover.

Schulz

Erich Schulz also produces convertibles. His program consists of a 2+2 two-door convertible. There are no other variants available in the standard program, which after all is not so unreasonable. The electro-hydraulically oper-

⬆ *Schulz: Convertible based on the Mercedes 190 (W 201).*

⬇ *Catori: Soft-top version based on Mercedes 190 (W 201).*

SKV: Semi-convertible based on the Mercedes 190 (W 201).

ated top is protected by a hard cover in the lowered position. Furthermore, all the windows can be completely lowered. The Schulz convertibles can be fitted with any of the accessories available from the comprehensive program of body styling parts. Finally, the firm offers a convertible with the six-cylinder or eight-cylinder engine. A car of this sort is no doubt a source of exquisite pleasure to the sports car fraternity, but at a cost of more than 100,000 marks, it is just about beyond reach and reason. The conversion of the bodywork, including all spraying, costs a good 40,000 marks just on its own. But so far as costs are concerned, it would be better to discuss matters with the makers, for fresh air driving with Mercedes is not exactly cheap—not even with the compact Mercedes.

Catori and SKV

The semi-convertible models produced by Catori are less complicated and expensive, as are those built by SKV. In these models, the side sections are left intact, with door frames, complete doors, and a section of roof frame over them. The soft top is then drawn up over the frame when it is not in the lowered position. The section of the soft top covering the front seats can be pulled up on its own, rather like a sliding roof, or removed entirely. This offers the fresh air fiend a variety of different options, while retaining the advantages of a semi-hardtop limousine. But the special feeling one has with a true convertible—both from the point of view of appearance and motoring—is missing with a car of this style.

However, the question of convertible or semi-convertible is not a problem. Anyone who enjoys fresh air driving would only consider a true convertible. If something more than just a sliding roof is required, without exposing oneself too much to the elements, especially in cold weather, then a semi-convertible would probably suffice—after all, a little fresh air is still better than none at all.

126

Schulz: Coupe based on the Mercedes 190 (W 201), with SEC-style bonnet.

Special bodywork

Where special bodywork for the Mercedes 190 is concerned, the styling companies are noticeably reticent. By comparison with the S-class models, there are no equivalent programs offering gullwing doors, chassis extensions, or station wagons. Only Chris Hahn, of the former Styling Garage in Pinneberg, is offering a "shrunken" version of the 190, known as City, with two doors, a drastically shortened chassis, a hat rack converted to serve as a loading surface, and a trunk. However, taking the projected conversion costs of 60,000 marks into consideration, it is likely to remain a one-off exercise.

So far, no styling companies have tackled a station wagon based on the Mercedes 190. If for no other reason, such a vehicle would be too similar to the factory T model of the old and new middle ranges (W 123/W 124).

And a sports car cum station wagon? It might be worth a prototype. But in view of the financial situation of many styling firms, it would be advisable to wait until a customer appears with a blank check in hand before a start is made on such a project.

Wheelbase extensions on the Mercedes 190 hardly make any sense, and even small pickups and delivery vans with a loading platform are hardly likely to find a buyer any more, except perhaps as vehicles for advertising or the like. Taken all in all, Erich Schulz has already produced the only truly realistic special body variant for the 190, a coupe variant.

This elegant and extremely restrained car could almost have been produced in this form by the factory in Stuttgart. Whether such an excellent car can really be taken up seriously or not, due to the heavy development costs and the amount of work involved in the conversion, is another matter over which there must be a large question mark. Nonetheless, at a very reasonable conversion cost of around 25,000 marks, a

127

Apal: Francorchamps front-engined sports car with the Mercedes 190 E2.3-16 or 190 E engine.

few coupes may well be built, which should recoup the investment.

On the other hand, it cannot be denied that Schulz has created something that cannot possibly be dismissed as primitive, juvenile, or not to be taken seriously, words that are frequently bandied about with some conversions. All too often, the detractors of modified or enhanced cars are inclined to damn them all for the sake of the erring few or accuse the firms in question of shoddy workmanship, but Schulz has nothing of this sort to fear with his coupe.

Complete cars
The manufacturers of complete cars based on the mechanical systems of a specific model—in this case, the Mercedes 190—go one step further than the manufacturers of special body shells.

So far, there are two makes that are based more or less completely on the mechanical systems of the 190, Apal and Isdera. Both are two-seater sports cars, but the overall concepts on which they are based are completely different.

Whereas Apal builds a front-engined sports car, the Francorchamps, with a massive box-type frame and very sizable dimensions (4400 × 1670 × 1240 mm), the Isdera Spider 033-16 is a thoroughbred mid-engined sports car with extravagant lines.

Parallels can be found between the two cars: Both have GRP bodywork and both makers use the same engine as the 190 E 2.3-16, which in its standard form produces 136 kW (185 hp). The top speed of the two cars would therefore be around 155 mph, with acceleration from 0 to 60 mph in about seven seconds.

Optionally, the basic model of the Apal is available with the standard 190 E engine, whose

Isdera: Mid-engined Isdera Spider 033-16 sports car with Mercedes 190 E 2.3-16 engine.

2.0-liter capacity produces 90 kW (122 hp). The Apal is also conceived along Targa lines, since the roof section can also be removed.

The driver of the Isdera Spider can enjoy even more fresh air. Without any roof at all, it is a pure fair-weather car, and therefore problematical in certain latitudes. On the other hand, it is designed through and through as a mid-engined sports car.

Both of these exotic cars, the Apal and the Isdera Spider, belong in the top price bracket—the Isdera actually exceeding the 100,000 mark limit.

For this reason alone, neither car is likely to sell in large numbers, but they are perfect examples of the changes taking place on the fringes of volume car production and will no doubt cause the hearts of many motorists to beat a little faster.

Finally, it is quite clear that the market for such a coupe must be relatively small. Although the Schulz coupe has been known to the public for some considerable time now and is regularly on display at motor shows, there are so far no signs of any rush to buy it.

Chapter 12

The new middle range—modern offensive

The successes achieved with the large S-class (W 126) and the compact Mercedes 190 series (W 201) have generally left the styling companies in a buoyant mood.

The inevitable happened: There was an enormous run on the first models of the new Mercedes middle range 200-300 E (W 124). Everyone wanted to get in first, and it was quite fascinating and scarcely credible in what a short space of time Brabus, Lorinser, MTS, or Schulz, for example, got their first models ready for photographing and testing.

The boom was particularly noticeable at the Frankfurt Motor Show (IAA) in 1985. Anyone who was conscious of his reputation and was not tied to a specific marque had a W 124 series Mercedes on display.

For some firms, it was this model that spurred them on to try their hand on Daimler-Benz cars for the first time—for example, the firm of Haslbeck.

The traditional companies involved in styling and enhancing Mercedes cars, such as AMG, Brabus, Duchatelet, Lorinser, and Schulz, already had complete or even excessively full programs on offer for the W 124. But the major volume manufacturers, BBS and Zender, were also already fully involved, and still are.

In the year since the new model appeared on the market, the styling program for the new Mercedes middle range has not yet reached the point where it is comparable in size to the 190 program, but the prospects for its doing so in the future are definitely bright.

Expensive enhancement projects, such as convertibles and wheelbase extensions, are not yet in development or are still at the prototype stage. Only Styling Garage (no longer in production) has already introduced a convertible version.

The reason for styling firms' reticence toward convertibles is that they are waiting for the new Mercedes W 124 series coupes.

The most ambitious project so far involving the new Mercedes middle range is the high-speed 124, produced by AMG. The reason their aim of building a car with a top speed of 186 mph was realized within such a short space of time was probably that AMG already had the most expensive and time-consuming component, the engine, already sitting on the shelf—a 5.6-liter V-8 thirty-two-valve S-class engine.

Adapting the huge engine to the rest of the mechanical systems of the W 124 was also very complicated and time-consuming, but even then it was easier than developing and testing a four-valve head from scratch.

Current programs

Body styling parts of plastic and interior enhancements can be ready for the market within the space of a few months. In the case of the W 124, everything proceeded even more rapidly and hectically. A number of the major Mercedes styling companies, such as Lorinser, had to have sizable quantities of preproduction spoilers produced by hand from GRP just to be among the first in the market, since production of metal molds for the foamed production parts would have taken several months longer.

Much the same applies to engine tuning, where Daimler-Benz has had a considerable influence on the attitudes of both manufacturers and purchasers. For internal reasons, only the 230 E was supplied to start with. The 260 E and 300 E came later. The tuners were not put out by this and merely raised the output of the 230 E engine to the level of the production model of the 260 E, or a little more. But after the first outcry and the hectic initial period among the tuning companies, common sense finally prevailed.

ABC

One firm that took a little longer over its development was ABC. But this company has now produced a standard version and an extremely wide one. The standard version comprises front and rear spoiler with bumpers and rocker panels, as well as a hood in the SEC style

and a freestanding rear wing à la factory sixteen-valve engine. ABC sells this car complete with special five-spoke rims made by the firm of Gotti.

And as with almost all styling firms, ABC will also lower the chassis if requested. In the case of the second, extremely wide version, this lowering is obligatory, as the chassis has been completely redesigned. Tires of the size of 285/40 R 15 on 10-inch rims have been fitted on the front and 345/35 R 15 on thirteen-inch rims on the rear—that is, the widest wheels currently available for use on the road. "Boots" of this size are provided on a production basis by the Lamborghini company for the Countach. In order to be able to accommodate these wheels on the W 124, various modifications were required to the chassis and wheelhouse. The bodywork inevitably increased considerably in width. The whole impression became somewhat exaggerated, particularly at the rear end, and very pronounced recesses were required in order for users to be able to get at the door handles.

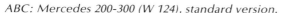

ABC: Mercedes 200-300 (W 124), standard version.

AMG: Mercedes 200-300 W 124 with adjustable front spoiler.

It must be admitted that not all these developments are rationally justified. They are the result of thinking purely in superlatives—on the part of both the stylists and the purchasers. If the widest version is in demand and can be marketed, then such a version has to be produced or else something similar created. Furthermore, one can assume that companies like ABC, for example, have done sufficient market research before undertaking such a development project.

AMG

With regard to the exterior, AMG is a little more restrained with its body styling parts. The company does not believe in wide bodies at any price, nor in boldly exaggerated dimensions. There are now two different sets of body styling and parts available from AMG for the Mercedes W 124. The second, newer version has been trimmed especially well to produce good drag and downpressure values. AMG's aim is to build

a limousine capable of a top speed of over 186 mph.

In their first model, the company offered a special front spoiler, the bottom half of which could be extended either by hand or by an electric motor, depending on the speed. This special feature, available on request, enables the spoiler to be kept at a respectable height for town driving in order not to catch on curbs and the like. When extended, the spoiler provides a large surface area, giving plenty of downpressure when driving at speed.

Technology involved is not so simple as it might at first appear, which is shown by the fact that the variable front spoiler is still not yet in serial production after over a year's development. There are problems associated not only with the smooth running of the operating mechanism at high speeds, questions of sealing, and damage resulting from minor accidents, but also with the enormously high price.

The rocker panels in the typical angular

AMG: Mercedes 200-300 (W 124) with 5.6-liter V-8 engine thirty-two-valve, C_d coefficient 0.25; aerodynamically speaking, this is the best of the standard limousines (top speed of 187 mph).

AMG style and the rear apron, on the other hand, are conventional in design. A flush-mounted or freestanding rear spoiler can be mounted on the trunk lid to round off the ensemble, at the purchaser's discretion.

The front spoiler of the high-speed version has partial underfloor paneling. Wind tunnel measurements were carried out with the prototype and resulted in a coefficient of drag of 0.25—an extraordinarily low figure, in fact the lowest such figure recorded for a limousine up to the time of publication (Spring 1985). Of particular interest is the statement from AMG that no special "lean tires" were fitted for the tests, that the rear mirror on the codriver's side was not removed, and that the radiator grille was not pasted over on the inside to prevent the airstream circulating round the engine compartment—all practices affecting the drag coeffi-

cient that are occasionally carried out by unscrupulous stylists to obtain more favorable test results.

Naturally, AMG will enhance the interior of the car as well. The finest woods, velours, leather, audio and video equipment, telephone, and much more besides can be supplied, all carefully matched by AMG. The list of extras here is long. Yet, whatever choice a purchaser makes, the result is a carefully and individuality styled interior that would whet the appetite of any purchaser.

The engines that provide the power for AMG's middle range models come with four levels of performance—for the time being, anyway. The basic version has an upgraded 2.3-liter four-cylinder unit taken from the 230 E, producing 118 kW (160 hp) at 5750 rpm with a maximum torque of 215 Nm at 4750 rpm. This performance

BBS: Mercedes 200-300 (W 124) with BBS lattice wheels.

is good enough to give a top speed of about 136 mph and acceleration from 0 to 60 in about nine seconds.

The next level is a 3.0-liter engine taken from the 300 E, which in AMG's hands is made to produce 165 kW (225 hp) at 6000 rpm and maximum torque of 282 Nm at 5000 rpm. Top speed of around 152 mph is entirely possible, coupled with acceleration from 0 to 60 in under eight seconds.

The third level is an enlarged 3.2-liter engine producing 180 kW (245 hp), for which a top speed of a good 155 mph can be assumed and acceleration from 0 to 60 in just over seven seconds.

The top of the engine range is a V-8 power unit taken from the S-class and fitted with four-valve cylinder heads developed by AMG. These massive units develop 250 kW (340 hp) from their five-liter capacity at 5750 rpm, while the 5.6-liter version of the unit produces 265 kW (360 hp) at 5500 rpm. The torque is equally colossal—457

Nm at 4500 rpm for the 5.0-liter version and 510 Nm at 4000 rpm for the 5.6-liter engine. Such an increase in engine output is not unnaturally accompanied by outstanding performance on the road. The five-liter AMG reaches 60 from a standing start in six seconds and will reach a top speed of 173 mph. The 5.6-liter version will just about reach the "sound barrier" of 186 mph and accelerate to 60 from a standing start in just on 5.5 seconds.

The price tag accompanying such cars is in keeping with their performance. AMG's top 124 model with the 5.6-liter four-valve engine costs about 120,000 marks and upward, depending on the final specification, for those with strong nerves and a good bank balance.

The AMG rims have come to take an important place in the overall styling program. Whereas the first, classical AMG rim, in Hans-Werner Aufrecht's words, was a variation on the Ferrari racing wheel, the two new rims are the result of translating the original five-spoke rim into the

Brabus: Mercedes 200-300 (W 124), $C_d = 0.26$.

aerodynamic age. They are noticeably independent in design and have a certain unmistakable style.

BBS

The firm of BBS offers a classical program of wheels for the "star among stars," consisting of two-piece and three-piece lattice wheels. They also offer a special kit for lowering the chassis and enhancing the bodywork, plus a spoiler set consisting of front spoiler, rocker panels, and rear apron. The aerodynamic parts are relatively restrained in design and do not need to be complemented by chassis modifications or changes of wheels.

Brabus

The bodywork conversion kit produced by Brabus for the middle-range Mercedes is also largely classical in appearance. Brabus claims to have achieved the best C_d value of any limousine in the world before AMG, namely 0.26, obtained with their version of the W 124 in 1985. In order to improve the aerodynamics, a front spoiler, rocker panels, and a rear apron were attached. This was complemented by a special swept-up trunk lid with a breakaway edge to control the airflow.

In addition to a comprehensive range of interior enhancements, including wood paneling, leather trim, and the usual special equipment such as stereo, video, and telephone, Brabus also supplies chassis modification and engine tuning kits for the four-cylinder and six-cylinder models.

Brabus does not quote a figure for the increased performance obtained from the four-cylinder engine, but in the case of the six-cylinder approximately 15 to 19 kW (20 to 25 hp) more power is said to have been achieved using classical tuning models.

Brinkmeyer

The firm of Brinkmeyer offers a middle-range Mercedes of rather eccentric style—a

Brinkmeyer: Mercedes 200-300 (W 124).

wide front spoiler with three large vents and an equally strange rear apron radically change the appearance of the Mercedes-Benz car. In the exhibition models, and those specially prepared for advertising photography, the add-on parts are in different color tones to the rest of the car, so that they are even more noticeable. More than with any other of the wide range of spoiler programs, the Brinkmeyer design is a question of the spontaneous taste of the individual.

Car Design Schacht

The conversion produced by Car Design Schacht gives the Mercedes 124 a very thickset appearance, as compared with the basic car with no spoilers added. At the same time, the very pronounced fender flair, in conjunction with the sharply inclined hood in the SEC style, makes this car look far more wedge-shaped than is the case with the factory model. In addition to the front spoiler, rear apron, rocker panels, fender flairs, and SEC-style hood, a trunk lid swept up in a restrained style and fitted with a breakaway edge or an enormous freestanding rear wing is also available for the middle-range Mercedes.

Naturally, Car Design Schacht has also made very considerable enhancements to the interior. These include the usual luxurious materials, such as fine woods, leather, and the like.

So far as the engine is concerned, the company provides turbocharged power units or, more recently, engines with mechanical compressors as an option.

Carlsson

The modified middle-range W 124 produced by Carlsson is very reminiscent of the initial car, the Mercedes 190. The front spoiler, rocker panels, and rear apron all show the same fluent style to which one has become accustomed with the compact Mercedes. This is complemented by the almost obligatory SEC hood with a wide radiator grille and a freestanding rear wing.

▲ *Car Design Schacht: Mercedes 200-300 (W 124).*   ▼ *Carlsson: Mercedes 200-300 (W 124).*

D + W: Mercedes 200-300 (W 124).

D + W

The Mercedes enhancement program developed by D + W, the major dealer in accessories, was also extended in the greatest haste to cover the 200-300 E. D + W has developed a kit consisting of front spoiler, rocker panels, rear apron, and freestanding rear wing. D + W also includes other makes of rims and chassis, taken from its own extensive mail-order warehouses.

Duchatelet

Belgium's well-known Mercedes modification and enhancement specialists, Duchatelet, has already extended its Carat by Duchtelet series to include the W 124. The bodywork styling program consists here too of front spoiler, rocker panels, and rear apron, as well as the ever more popular restrained and freestanding rear wing. In the firm's usual way, Duchatelet has taken particular care with the design of the inte-

rior. High-quality wood panels, leather as far as the eye can see, or velour if preferred, thick carpeting, top-quality entertainment ranging from audio to video—all of this is available for the Mercedes 124 from Duchatelet if one can afford the not inconsiderable prices involved. Apart from adding new wheels and installing another chassis, Duchatelet steers clear of all mechanical changes.

Haslbeck

The firm of Haslbeck is based in Muhldorf on the Inn, close to the Austrian border. This firm—like Duchatelet—is very cautious where mechanical modifications are concerned. They have done a great deal of business with accessories that they have developed and manufactured themselves, especially for cross-country vehicles and Japanese volume-produced cars; in some cases they were working directly for the Japa-

Duchatelet: Mercedes 200-300 (W 124).

nese manufacturers' dealer organizations and the parts were illustrated in the sales brochures. However, where the Mercedes middle-range models are concerned, Haslbeck is getting embroiled in a hotly competitive market.

The add-on parts are stylishly designed in keeping with the production model of the 190 E 2.3-16, though they are not all that distinctive compared with their competitors. Added to that, Haslbeck is not exactly timid in its pricing, and for that reason alone, the company will not find it easy to gain a foothold in this market. The Haslbeck 124 has a front spoiler of its own design, rocker panels, rear apron, and a free-standing wing that continues along the top of the rear fender. It is fitted with relatively smooth-surfaced rims, completely in the style of the factory sixteen-valve model.

HF

The HF body styling kit has a style all of its own. Front spoiler and door panels have a broad grooved profile and largely determine the appearance of the styling parts. The front spoiler also has the typcial trapezoidal apertures that can be used either for additional headlamps or for channels to funnel air to the brakes. The rear apron and SEC-style hood complete the program. Due to the eye-catching grooved design, the 124 with HF styling parts reminds one of the SEC coupe during the days when the door panels of the factory models were similarly grooved.

Koenig Specials

Koenig Specials, the styling specialists based in Munich, has also recently taken the 124 in hand and is offering a spoiler set and wide wheels, for instance 245/45 at the rear.

Lorinser

Lorinser, one of the pioneers and market leaders among the Mercedes stylists, was one of

Haslbeck: Mercedes 200-300 (W 124).

the first to set to work on the Mercedes-Benz middle-range models. The first model was barely on the market when the first test cars were available to display the styling parts. In the meantime, Lorinser not only has sold a great many of these parts but also has extended the program considerably. The second, wider version is now also available to add to the narrower standard version: Its program, in the same style as that for the standard version, similarly consists of front spoiler, rocker panels, and rear apron, whereby the rocker panels, which provide the transition to the extended rear fenders, are extended further to the rear. The same applies to the rear apron. A freestanding wing à la 190 E 2.3-16 can be added as well.

The Lorinser program is augmented by two rims of its own design. Whereas the first of these, which has already been available for some time, reminds one of the factory design, the new single-rim, or optional three-part rim, is a smooth-surfaced unornamented five-spoke creation.

Lotec

The firm of Lotec, near Rosenheim, is still more or less in the process of building up its program. At the present time, the company is offering a styling program for the standard Mercedes 124 models. In addition to the very restrained plastic styling parts, consisting of front spoiler, rocker panels, and rear apron, there is also an SEC-like hood or a special hood in the style of the original in which the radiator grille is an integral part of the GRP hood, instead of being installed separately as in the production models. This is a modern and dynamic alternative to the SEC hood, since the original appearance has largely been retained. The engine has been provided with a mechanical compressor to charge up the three-liter power unit. Planned output is of the order of 198 to 220 kW (270 to 300 hp).

MTS

The firm of MTS was also one of the first to enter the market with a program of bodywork

Lorinser: Mercedes station wagon (Model T, W 124) with Lorinser rims.

styling parts for the middle-range Mercedes cars. The MTS kit differs relatively sharply from those of its chief rivals, being very much in the style of its 190 kit; it comprises a front spoiler, which blends very well with the overall appearance of the limousine, smooth-surfaced door panels, rocker panels with clean lines, which merge into the applied fender extensions, and a restrained rear apron. The whole ensemble is crowned with a freestanding rear wing of arbitrary and angular design, which nevertheless fits well into the MTS bodywork styling kit. MTS also modifies chassis and fits different wheels.

Schulz

The firm of Schulz was a pioneer among styling companies where the 190 is concerned, leading the way in three different sectors: convertibles, five-liter engines, and coupes. Where

the 124 is concerned, however, major innovations have so far not appeared. In spite of that, Erich Schulz has still managed to be one of the first in the field with his bodywork styling kit. This gave one the impression of trying to make the new middle-range W 124 look like the old middle-range W 123. The structured bumper area with front spoiler and rear apron remind one of the previous model, as does the lower part of the rear apron, which quickly recedes under the car. Schulz has added a considerable degree of rounding and ornamentation to the new, smooth-surfaced straight-line image of the aerodynamic generation. The freestanding rear wing and the hood in the SEC style conform, however, with the general picture.

The Schulz triangle in fluted colored plastic, designed to supplement the trapezoidal rear lights (which took a lot of getting used to, at least in the early days, and were commonly called "cheese segments") is so far quite unique. This

Lorinser: Mercedes 200-300 (W 124) wide version with Lorinser rims.

Schulz: Mercedes 200-300 (W 124).

Vestatec: Mercedes 200-300 (W 124) with small SEC radiator panel mounted on the front.

too is reminiscent of the other, older Daimler-Benz series. The Schulz 124, complete with its spoilers, thus looks more well-behaved and normal than those products of its competitors that have all the attributes of the normal limousine and take so much getting used to.

However, things get a little less well-behaved when Schulz adds turbocharging to the 2.3-liter engine. This results in an output of 138 kW (190 hp) at 5100 rpm to drive the wedge-shaped Mercedes forward with a maximum torque of 205 Nm at 3500 rpm and a maximum speed of just over 142 mph. Acceleration from 0 to 60 is about 8.5 seconds.

Vestatec
The unusual feature of the Vestatec 124 is the SEC-like radiator grille, which is installed in place of the original screen. This is not an SEC-modified hood, only a considerably cheaper

means of adding an SEC-style touch to the 124, but no doubt there will be plenty of owners who balk at the idea of paying 3,000 to 3,500 marks for a hood in the SEC style and would be prepared to settle for a halfway solution at a fifth of the price. Otherwise, the Vestatec set is entirely conventional, consisting of fluted front spoiler, straight-line rocker panels, and a well-proportioned freestanding rear wing.

Zender
Zender's designer, Zillner, has created for the new middle-range Mercedes an elegant spoiler kit, which is characterized by clean lines. The front spoiler, rocker panels, door panels, and rear apron blend most harmoniously with the overall picture of the Mercedes bodywork. Everything fits together harmoniously and unobtrusively. The whole ensemble is rounded off by a flat freestanding rear wing, mounted very low

Zender: Mercedes 200-300 (W 124) with Zender rims.

over the trunk lid, and massive rims in Zender's new design, which underline the dynamic qualities and the solidity of the overall bodywork.

A piece of nostalgia

From the above description of the programs of the various styling companies one can see that there are already a wide variety of modified and enhanced models available on the market for the W 124—in short, something for everybody.

The sort of modifications that have so far, surprisingly, been conspicuous by their absence are the wholesale conversions, such as convertibles and wheelbase extensions.

The firm of GFG, however, did spring one surprise. This specialist company, producing security vehicles and wheelbase extensions, developed a semi-replica of an older Mercedes model based on the W 124. This is very reminiscent of the 540 K sports car of the years prior to World War II. The Elisar, with its long hood, gently curving fenders, and wire spoke wheels, reminds one of the long-lost luxury of the days when many cars were still hand-built creations produced for the chosen few and when it was all part of the good breeding expected of aristocrats that they had their cars built by hand by a special coachbuilder. Only the chassis and engine were provided by the car factory. The remainder, that is the bodywork and the interior, was designed by the coachbuilder and the client together.

Today, it would be impossible to pay for such an order, given the present rates of pay, for thousands of hours of labor went into the hand-crafting wood, metal, and glass. The Elisar recreated this touch—in a diluted and nostalgic form of course—using a three-liter engine taken from the 300 E of the new middle-range models, the whole thing costing 165,000 marks.

GFG: Elisar model, a replica based on W 124 technology, in the style of the 1930's and modeled on the 540 K.

What's next?

The big surprise in the styling lottery: So far, there is no convertible based on the new Daimler-Benz middle-range models—with just one exception. The main reason for this is probably that, on the basis of press information, the entire branch had reckoned on the impending sale of the 124 coupe, which has since been announced. The only convertible known so far, the one produced by the former Styling Garage, has indeed been produced as a prototype limousine, but at the same time it was announced that it would go into final production as a coupe.

Four doors were therefore changed to two, at considerable expense, the back of the car around the rear window was modified, and a convertible soft top was developed that looks as though it were a substitute for the metal roof of a coupe. Although the ex-works price of the coupe will be considerably higher than that of the limousine, the difference will probably be balanced out by the difference between four doors and two.

Whether it really makes sense in the final analysis to build a four-door convertible version based on the 124, in the same way as the Swiss firm Caruna is doing with the S-class, is more than debatable. So there is no likelihood of any convertible before the factory coupe appears on the market.

And what would happen if Daimler-Benz itself were to offer a two-door convertible based on the coupe, as happened before with the old S class? In view of the worldwide boom in convertible sales and the ambitions nurtured by BMW in that direction, could it be just idle speculation?

The styling fraternity would then again be in a position where the all-powerful manufacturers would be snatching away beneath their very noses a piece of cake that they had baked themselves. And all produced better, more perfectly and—in the interest of the customers—more cheaply, with factory servicing and warranties. But again coupled with the loss of a bit more individuality and craftsmanship! The small bodywork specialists would have to look elsewhere for business.

Any possibility of gullwing cars will have to wait—if it comes about at all—until the factory coupe makes its appearance.

The question still remains of whether customers will choose the well-tried and tested SEC version straight away, given the fantasy prices asked for the exotic versions in question.

The station wagon version, of which a very few were built, based on the S-class models, is also a dead duck where the middle-range is concerned since they are already available ex-works.

So what is left over for the "metal bashers"?

The imperial sedan, that is, the extended wheelbase version of the limousine, would offer some scope. Built in numerous designs based on the S class, and even popular as taxis or airport transporters when based on the old middle-range W 123, it would not be so easy to realize with the new middle-range models. It is no longer sufficient to insert an additional section in the middle, due to the pronounced wedge-shaped bodywork. In order to retain the side line, considerable retouching is required merely to ensure that there are no "kinks" in the rising lines.

An extended version, based on the station wagon, would be conceivable and perhaps easier to put into effect. However, a car of this sort with the station wagon rear end would lack the worldwide appeal of other models.

A car based on the T-model series would also be conceivable, with a superstructure designed for use as a large-capacity vehicle, lux-ury trailer, or even traveling conference room. Perhaps the most suitable form, with an additional axle and all-wheel drive, would be that of a playboy's traveling "pad."

Perhaps Franco Sbarro, the great Swiss producer of ideas, has already inspired one of his colleagues to build a double gullwing 124 based on the limousine version. Who knows?

Whether such projects could be realized or not is not a decision for the manufacturer alone, who would be well advised to reach agreement with the customer on advance financing of the project.

One of the most probable scenarios is the building of complete bodyworks based on the outstanding current Daimler-Benz chassis and mechanical systems. The excellent chassis and the modern engine technology almost cry out for a body built more on racing car lines, whether in the form of nostalgic replicas of former Mercedes sports cars or as present-day road racers.

Chassis and engines, suitably trimmed and tuned, especially using mechanical compressors, will help individually produced or small-series sports cars to achieve tremendous performance and first-class characteristics comparable with the very best sports cars. Outputs of 220 kW (300 hp) and top speeds of around 185 mph would certainly be in the cards.

Seen in this light, prices of 150,000 to 250,000 marks would not be unrealistic, since other companies, such as, for example, Lamborghini, Ferrari, Aston Martin, and Porsche, are asking that sort of price or even more.

Top speeds of 185 mph on the road will therefore become the magic figure for tuners working on the Mercedes 124 series.

The firm of AMG has already reached this goal with a great deal of effort and at enormous cost. This was expended not exclusively in connection with the new Mercedes middle-range, but for the most part it went into the development of the five-liter or 5.6-liter V-8 four-valve engine for the S class. The output levels had to be adjusted for the 124 and the entire transmission and mechanical systems on the chassis adjusted to suit that. This was no easy task, especially where the rear axle and gearbox, which derived in part from the S class, were concerned.

Not all styling and tuning firms have the resources that AMG has at its command. In most cases, they have to find ways and means of achieving the same goal with less effort and expense.

Apart from any sudden unforeseeable flashes of inspiration, the general panacea for the next generation of motorists is likely to be the mechanical compressor. Styling and tuning companies everywhere are talking in these terms, and the automobile industry itself has already put it into practice in a number of special or small-series models such as the Lancia Volumex versions, the Opel Comprex series, or the VW Polo range.

The benefits of the mechanical compressor, technically speaking, are to be found in the con-tinuous increase in output from idling speed onward, the absence of any delayed response when accelerating, and the considerably lower engine temperature. The true reason, however, from the tuner's point of view is that approximately the same output can be achieved at considerably lower cost. These savings, as compared with the turbo, will not all be passed on to the customer in the early stages. Only when all the tuning firms have concentrated their efforts on the new technology will it become clear that prices can be kept considerably lower than those for turbocharger versions of approximately the same level of performance.

Another area to which tuners and stylists may devote considerable interest and attention in the future is the electronically controlled chassis. Here again AMG has taken on the role of pioneer, though only in respect of the S class.

Styling Garage: Convertible based on the 200-300 (W 124).

However, it is to be expected that this or similar technology will be transferred by AMG or some other firm to the middle-range Mercedes models, the firm having first tried it out thoroughly in the S class.

Another special market sector of interest to the tuners and stylists could be the new communications technology. Adapted to meet the needs of managers, lawyers, doctors, tax consultants, entrepreneurs, and even pop stars and others under similar stress, it should soon be possible, not only to flood the car with music from the ether, CD discs, video, and cassette, but also to communicate directly with the office, the stock exchange, clients, patients, friends, and relations. The whole thing comes down to a total information society, which wants to have the very latest advances in telephone, teletext, telecopier, video, and television technology, not only in the home or the office but also in the hotel or, as in this case, out and about in the car.

On a detailed level, these systems will make it possible for the manager or boss of a company to access the latest information stored in the office. In this way, the boss can keep absolutely up to date on all developments and all matters concerning orders, bank balances, personnel matters, complaints, and the like, at any time of the day or night, without having to actually talk to any member of the staff. In the same way, his wife can leave messages on the home computer, if she had to go to the hairdresser's or if the children have got bad marks, or if she wants her husband to bring a bottle of champagne with him because it is her birthday.

The sort of problems that such developments can bring with them concern licenses for linking up with telephone and radio networks, plus data security to prevent unauthorized access to data stored on computer systems, for example, in a law firm.

All in all, one can expect that, in accordance with the general trend, the development of sporting, specifically adapted, and serious styling packages will be in the forefront of interest with specific regard to the 124.

There is likely to be less interest shown by oil-rich sheiks and wealthy pop stars and more by well-off—or not so well-off—businesspeople who like to travel faster in comfort and style, avoiding stress. They want to have the feeling that they have done something for their own health too, especially since they spend a lot of time in their cars.

Chapter 13

S for superclass

With Mercedes, in general, being widely acclaimed a king among car manufacturers, the imperial honors must go to the S class. Indeed, since entering the market, this series has come to be recognized as the ultimate money can buy.

The men of Stuttgart are, of course, well pleased with the worldwide acclaim of the S class; but even the dollar-affluent conversion specialists are beadily eyeing this masterpiece of German automobile engineering.

Now, with this status symbol clearly beyond the reach of ordinary checkbooks, the uninitiated may well wonder why production cars should be modified at all.

They're missing the point.

Ever known anybody to be content with what he has? For the well-heeled S-class clientele, merely driving the best isn't good enough: You must also be seen doing it; if everybody can see you can afford it, you must be doing well. In certain circles at least, envying and being envied are but a very short step apart.

When firms like AMG and Lorinser, concurrently with the debut of the new S class in 1979, embarked on an intensive postproduction cosmetic change program, there were quite a few to whom this didn't make any sense at all. Wrong again!

Just as the latest S class did away with the chromium-plated glitter of its predecessors, so a new class of customers appeared on the horizon after an extended interlude, complaining about plastic lateral door weather strips and unconventional trendy and sporty styling on the great

Daimler-Benz series models: The Stuttgart flagship became a smoothly elegant conversion overnight. There can be little doubt that, as in so many instances of outstanding financial successes, the accidental choice of exactly the right point in time played a major role.

Here, the new limousine with the cool, sleek looks entered the market precisely at the time when young looks and a dynamic lifestyle were "in," especially with the high-income-bracketed 35-to-50 age groups. It also became obvious that good aerodynamics were conducive not only to improving S-class sales figures (even at times when gas prices were rising astronomically) but also to generating, thanks to an overall concept of engine, chassis, bodywork, and interior, an acceptance of outstanding technological capability. This in turn enabled the new dynamic clientele to justify the purchase of an "old-fashioned" automobile.

With the S class, a single automobile version, Daimler-Benz succeeded in bringing about a dramatic change from the "cloth-cap" image to "car of young dynamic achievers," cars aiming either at the same, albeit less affluent, clientele or at second and third car owners who might previously have driven a Golf GTI, a No. 3 BMW, or a similar vehicle.

And so it came to pass that AMG, Lorinser, and others found a receptive market waiting for their attractive package. It comprised, first, a clientele that wanted something better, something more exclusive. Conversions involved engine, chassis, and modifications of outside and interior features; they were always carried out selectively and in good taste.

The pioneers of Daimler-Benz conversions, first and foremost AMG and Lorinser, have remained faithful to their original styling and target clientele. The latter consists mainly of successful businessmen who like to have fun with their automobiles and attach importance to a well-balanced image that unobtrusively sets them apart from the rest: Customized rims and one or two extras are as far as they will go. Unobtrusive fender modifications or an SEC hood on a limousine will then become Cloud Nine.

The low-key takeoff of the conversion program was followed by more spectacular developments. The oil price explosion, followed—albeit with some delay—by a similarly rocketing rate of exchange of the US dollar, attracted a clientele of millionaires and billionaires whose interests were diametrically opposed to those of previous Mercedes customers.

What they wanted was blatant ostentation and never mind the expense!

Superlatives, for starters! The longest SEL, the most expensive SEC, the widest SEC, gull-wing doors on the SEC (more recently even four on the SEL variant) cabriolets, golden fittings, hood styling on Mercedes 600 lines, sophisticated onboard catering facilities, the lot!

To accommodate the new clientele, a number of firms specialized—if only temporarily—in conversions on these lines. First and foremost was the former Styling Garage, located at Pinneberg near Hamburg, where supercars, known as Oil Sheik Cunarders, went into production. Other firms jumped on the bandwgon.

When the first symptoms of weakening of the dollar in the Arab and US markets were diagnosed, quick action to stem at least some of the worst excesses was imperative. New markets were found, albeit no longer as lucrative and productive as before, for example, Japan, Latin America, United Kingdom, Spain, Hong Kong, Malaysia, Australia, and South Africa. This reorientation, however, brought about a dramatic drop of conversion costs from madhouse levels of 300,000 marks as maximum to the by comparison modest 100,000 to 200,000 marks. Further-

more, every customer had to be fought for. Some firms, having experienced setbacks one way or another, reduced their prices by as much as half merely to remain in business.

The content of the third, most recently launched, stage of the Mercedes conversion program can be roughly summarized as follows: Europe-oriented wide-body design, matched with any desired power unit under the hood, as required. Prime examples: the wide-body SEC and SEL versions from Koenig Specials of Munich, with maximum 294 kW (400 hp), shortly to be increased to 367 kw (500 hp) on the 5.6-liter engine. These conversions will set buyers back 40,000 marks for outside trim and paintwork customizing, 40,000 marks for an "engine power boost package," and the same figure for roof restructuring. Anyone with money to spare who is intent on spending it is at liberty to pay a few thousand marks on interior restyling. Conversions costing more than these figures, nobody would want to know about.

With one exception, though, as in so many other areas of human activity, fear will always generate business. There is a ready market for armor-plating and security glazing on automobiles, frequently with the resultant need for Pullman-type chassis extensions, for heads of state, crowned or otherwise. Others need extra floor space for rear seats.

To these options should be added the steel-sheet-roof versions, of which a few are still around. Nobody else being interested, the conversion specialists took over and turned the veterans into cabrios.

Reference is also needed to the amazing Extra-Super Sports Specials with Daimler-Benz V-8 engines. Their fans, a comprehensive mix, from former bodywork glamour fanatics to adherents of advanced technology applications, obviously have lost interest in sedate US mass-produced versions and have turned to stargazing instead. Gazing at a star atop an engine, for example!

Interior trim and fittings, comprising mainly curtains, seat covers, TV, and bar facilities, rather like a powder room or high-class pub on wheels, have meanwhile also reverted to more conven-

ABC: Mercedes 500 SEC (W 126) wide-body version.

tional patterns. There is a general bias in favor of a more sober, technologically minded outlook. In place of a bar there are minirefrigerators and small folding tables and in the place of a television, minicomputers with multifunction screen and built-in video capability.

S class conversion therefore covers an impressive multipurpose package that is beyond comparison.

Styling and structural conversions
ABC

Daimler-Benz S class conversions are the specialized business activity of ABC-Exclusive, Mercedes conversion experts located at Bonn. ABC's first venture in this field was a four-seat cabrio, which was exhibited at the 1983 Frankfurt Automobile Show (IAA). Since then, the ABC program for the big Mercedes range has been extended to practically anything marketable.

The program starts with a spoiler package for limousines and coupes: Front spoiler, rocker panels with wheelhouse extension, and rear skirt can be supplemented by a freestanding rear wing on 190 four-valve version lines. And to cater to those who really want to be noticed, there is the ABC wide-body version, albeit available for the coupe only. The external appearance of the package is determined by Rippen's boldly ornamental front spoilers and lateral parts. Add to all this the enormous protruding rear wing and a hood blister, and there will be little left of the sedate elegance of the original. The ABC wide version obviously calls for a correspondingly advanced tire concept, with the 345/35 R 15 rear tires as absolute limit. Rims to match the tires are of the ABC-marketed French Gotti type.

ABC is, of course, also concerned with the interiors of Daimler's star performer. Using mainly leather, mohair wool, sheepskin, wood paneling, and gold plating, a new interior ambiance has been created. There are also the conventional extras—bars, stereo, video systems, and the like. Apart from chassis conversions, ABC will also fit five-speed sports or overdrive systems in the place of standard automatic transmissions.

AMG

Basic AMG philosophy aims at presenting its clientele with customized automobiles, assembled to individual requirements. Hans-Werner Aufrecht, head of the company, has at all times endeavored to inject more than a modicum of sporty behavior and a taste for driving pleasure into his products, as witnessed first and foremost on the big Mercedes versions. The Stuttgart-based firm of styling specialists has managed, incredibly, to develop a four-cylinder head assembly complete with all necessary arrangements for integration into the engine block. With V-8 thirty-two valves, the heavy limousine matches top-class sports car performance data. The 5.6-liter engine, producing 265 kW (360 hp) at 5500/min, together with the enormous torque of 510 Nm at 4500/min, enables the 100 km/h mark to be reached from a standing start in six seconds flat, with the powerful thrust not reaching its maximum before the 270 km/h mark.

Other AMG tuning programs for the S class produce more modest results. The program starts with a five-liter two-valve configuration, producing 203 kW (276 hp) at 5750/min and 408 Nm at 4000/min torque; the car will accelerate from 0 to 100 km/h in approximately 7.5 seconds, with maximum speed in the region of 240 km/h. The 5.4-liter two-valve version, with 228 kW (310 hp) at 5350/min and 475 Nm at 4000/min torque, takes less than seven seconds from zero to 100 km/h, with maximum speed approximately 250 km/h.

The five-liter four-valve version, producing 250 kW (340 hp) at 5750/min, with maximum 547 Nm at 4500/min torque, follows in second place for engine power. This capability enables a maximum speed of 260 km/h to be attained, acceleration from standing start to 100 km/h taking 6.5 seconds.

Modifications can, however, also be made

ABC: Mercedes 500 SEC interior (cabriolet version).

AMG: Mercedes 560 SEL (W 126) with V-8 thirty-two-valve engine and computer-controlled damper setting.

to the external appearance of S-class cars. AMG, one of the first firms to restyle bodywork on the new S class, has since then developed a near-standarized image of all Daimler-Benz models. Since the introduction of its conversion kit for the new mid-range (W 124), the S-class kit has also been modified. Most obvious and typically S class are the square-cut side trim panels, which are largely a matter of personal taste. Conversely, front spoiler and rear skirt design is very conservative. The trunk lid has been fitted with a rear spoiler. These parts can be used on limousines and coupes. Fender extensions, although suitable for SEC coupes only, no longer have huge bulbous ends as used by other firms. Wheel dimensions, at 225/50 R 16, remain within very reasonable limits.

AMG's philosophy on interior conversions is the same as for engine tuning and external appearance. In line with traditional Stuttgart principles, AMG's aim is technical perfection without ostentation and with inconspicuous

detail features for the benefit of passengers. Only the best materials are used for all the work carried out.

AMG provides two special chassis items. First are the two special AMG rims. The older of the two, with five robust radial spokes, is already well known. The other, an aerodynamically shaped modern type, is characterized by a super-smooth finish.

The company's range also includes a computer-controlled chassis synchronization system, incorporating automatic pull and push control when the car is moving. The device is governed by speed, lateral inclination, and load. Provision is made for manual preselection of three damping steps as basic setting.

For brisk driving, the suspension control will always be automatically set on maximum firmness to ensure optimal road-holding at high speeds or with significant transverse acceleration through bends under power. This chassis is available, as a CD chassis, exclusively for S-class

154

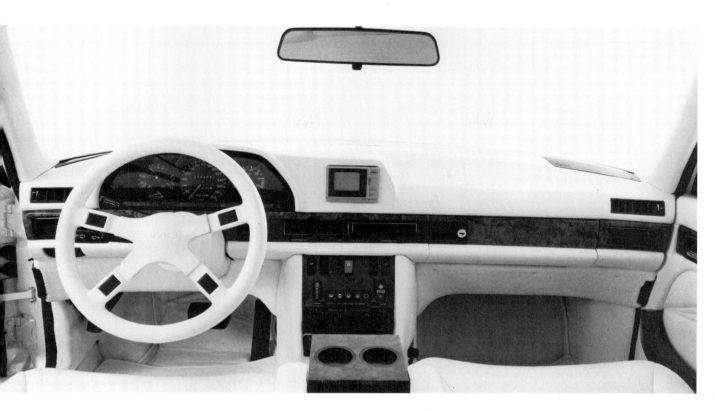

◆ *AMG: Interior.*

◆ *AMG: Mercedes SEC series (W 126) wide-body version.*

Benny S: PanAm on Mercedes 500 SEC (W 126) basic design.

cars (CD stands for "computer-controlled damper configuration").

Benny S-Car

Benny S-Car builds a head-turning machine named PanAm, based on the SEC coupe, with sports oversize fender extensions. Wheels have 345/35 R 15 tires, the fattest permissible on public highways, mounted on thirteen-inch rims. Overall modifications made to the appearance of the SEC coupe are such as to completely set it apart from the vehicles of other conversion specialists. This image is unlikely to please everybody, as it is diametrically opposed to the general spoiler trend.

Dominant feature of the Benny S version is the front spoiler, its off-beat design matching the tubby macho-inspired fender extensions. The rather low-key look of the rocker panels is

effectively balanced by the chunky fender extensions, giving the impression that the wheels protrude outward beyond the bodywork. Front spoiler design is unusual, with the rounded outline and drawn-in mid-front section underscoring its compromising image.

Finally, Benny S-Car also carries out conversions similar to those of other restyling specialists, for example, lowering chassis assembly and uprating modifications to the car's interior.

Bickel Tuning

For the big Daimler-Benz class SE, SEL, and SEC models, front spoilers, rocker panels, and rear skirts are also available from Bickel Tuning. Rocker panels are supplied complete with narrow fenders. Basically, however, the Boschert-designed Bickel program remains within low-key limits.

Bickel: Mercedes SEC series (W 126).   *Brabus: Mercedes 500 SEC (W 126).*

Brabus: Interior.

Brabus

Brabus' comprehensive program is backed by more extensive experience: The Bottrop-based conversion specialists form part of the Auto Buschmann group, whose main business is Daimler-Benz private car marketing. Brabus Autosport consequently soon became actively interested in the S class and eventually developed a bodywork program for limousines and coupes whose main features are reflected in construction kits for the remaining Daimler-Benz models. The standard program comprises front spoilers, rocker panels, and rear skirts. Visual impact, however, is rather low-key, and this is a good point, since the construction kit is easily compatible with standard rims.

SEC-style hoods and spoiler breakaway edges on trunk cover plates, a layout also popular with firms like Lorinser, are optionally available for limousines. Brabus will exchange standard chassis and wheels for special designs.

These parts originate from standard programs of other accessory manufacturers.

Brabus specialities include macho-sounding twin and quadruple exhaust systems.

S class engine tuning is by means of compressors or turbochargers. Capacity ranges from 206 to 235 kW (280 to 320 hp).

In common with other conversion specialists, Brabus is keenly interested in uprating the interiors of cars, using high-grade wood, leather, and other luxury-class materials. Optional extras range from audio and video systems to bar facilities.

D + W

D + W is an accessory wholesaler that supplies a range of parts required for uprating Daimler-Benz S-class aerodynamics programs. Parts styling is based on the original pattern first applied to S-class (W 126) cars. Groove taping is

◆ *D + W: Mercedes SEC series (W 126).*   ◆ *Duchatelet: Mercedes S class (W 126).*

Duchatelet: Interior.

freely used on parts, with front spoilers, rocker panels, and door trim panels, together with a slim rear skirt forming a complete kit. SEC hoods for limousines and cutaway-edge trunk cover plates are, of course, available as optional extras.

D + W's general accessory program comprises wheels and chassis, and also in-house-designed plain rims.

Duchatelet

To classify the spoiler kit of the Belgian upmarket tuning specialist, Duchatelet, as unobtrusive would be an understatement. Indeed, unless an original S-class model of 1986 vintage happened to stand next to one of Duchatelet's conversions, the difference would hardly be noticeable. Front spoiler, rocker panels, and rear skirt have been integrated into the overall shape so smoothly and unobtrusively that they become part of the bodywork. By contrast, the appearance of Duchatelet's previous construction kit was much more obtrusive and also designed on much less harmonious lines.

Duchatelet's particular forte is the solid elegance underlying his interior conversions. He shuns coarse and blatant ostentation inside the car. There are no falcon-headed gear shifters, gold or gold-plated trim panels, no superfluous electronic gadgets. Instead, color-matching hide and velour upholstery, thick floor carpets, and carefully balanced wood paneling dominate the interior. Duchatelet will, of course, also accommodate customers who prefer more ostentations and less conservative color schemes and accessories. Comply he will. His style, however, is not for sale.

Gemballa

An encounter with Gemballa's overwidth SEC coupe is of the more unusual kind. For a number of years the young Leonberg company

160

specialized—at least so far as outside appearance is concerned—exclusively in Porsche cars. However, it has expanded to include Daimler-Benz products, Gemballa's SEC coupe—Daimler's prestige machine—now making its debut. With its massive tires, 225/50 R 15 (front) and 345/35 R 15 (rear), the thoroughbred newcomer will hardly be found to be under-tired. Tires are mounted on Ronal rims, with wheels fitting under chunky fender extensions. Measured over the rear wheels, this impressive automobile has an overall dimension in the region of two meters, mainly due to the rear extensions with cooling slots. Toward the front, these extensions merge gradually with the side skirts, while rearward they run into the spoiler, starting some considerable distance away in the side member. The clean, smooth appearance of all fitted parts can be taken for granted. That the company, rather than succumbing to the current Testarossa epidemic, has managed to give the rear extension air vents an image of its own also speaks in its favor; nor should the idea of a laterally positioned rear spoiler be underestimated.

So far as exterior appearance is concerned, Gemballa still hasn't joined the wide-body SEC avant-garde. Quite likely he had no such intentions and wanted to meet customers' tastes. Nothing wrong with that; after all, conversion specialists also want to eat . . .

As indicated by the company's name, Gemballa Automobilinterieur GmbH (Automobile Interior Ltd.), Gemballa had from the outset paid attention to S-class interior modifications. Apart from Gemballa specials, for example, steering-wheel-controlled audio systems, high-grade upholstery, and superb interior design, Gemballa has recently introduced a rear-window video system featuring a scan camera integral with the mirror casing, projecting the rear-view image onto a miniscreen in the dash, so that the driver can see what is happening behind the car.

True, such refinements can be regarded as superfluous gadgets, especially with the price, 12,000 marks, no doubt on the high side. It will be interesting to see whether a production car manufacturer latches on to Gemballa's idea and is prepared to fit the appliance in larger quantities; costs could then be reduced to a fraction of

present levels, possibly to around 2000 to 3000 marks. Eventually, with a simplified system and cheaper components, even lower prices could become practical.

GFG

GFG mainly builds carbrios and security vehicles (discussed elsewhere in greater detail) but it also provides a range of conventional body conversion parts. For the S class, these parts comprise front spoiler, skirts under rocker panels, and rear skirt. GFG also caters for conventional requirements, for example, suspension lowering, special rims, and the like.

Finally, GFG is licensed to fit three-liter diesel engines to S-class limousines.

Looking at the S-class construction kit, any doubts regarding the origin of the basic concept underlying all HF designs will be quickly dispelled. The front spoiler will be identified as a continuation of the wide grooved band on original production door panels. This configuration was subsequently applied to the 190, the 200 to 300 E series, and the SL variant by way of in-house identification. There is a matching rear skirt and, as an optional extra, a hood, based on SEC design, for limousines.

Kamei

Kamei, Germany's well-known spoiler pioneer, obviously could not distance himself from the S-class conversion kit market and can supply reasonably priced front spoilers, rocker panels, and rear skirts for this category. The range is complemented by Kamei's badge kit, which leaves onlookers in no doubt whatever as to what spoiler is taking this particular S-class limo for a ride.

Konig

The seat manufacturer Konig is a newcomer in the S-class conversion market. Extra-extrovert styling characterizes the conversion kit, compris-

▲ GFG: Long wheelbase Mercedes S class (W 126).   ▼ Kamei: Mercedes S class (W 126).

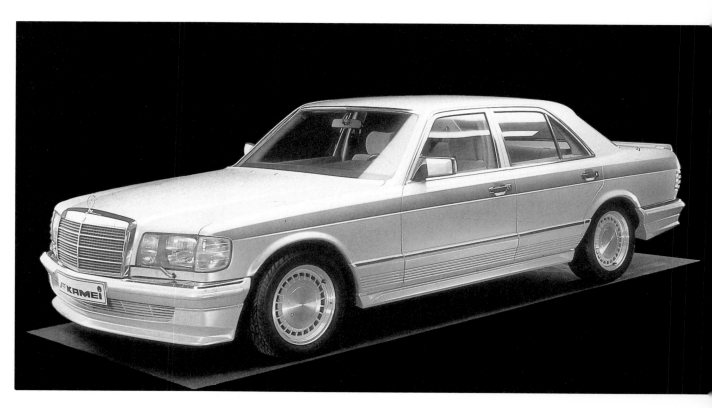

HF: Mercedes S class (W 126).

ing front spoiler, rocker panels, and rear skirt. Below bumper level, the front spoiler has odd-looking small vents, extending over the whole width of the car, continuing along the side into the fender. In front of the rear wheels, air ducts all but merge with the side skirts. A notable feature of the rear skirt is the integrated number plate, positioned below bumper level, the vacant space being taken up by a red transparent insert piece between the rear lamp assemblies. The boot lid can be provided with a spoiler, extending laterally past the fenders all the way to the front.

Konig's activities also cover interior work. In addition to standard video sets, bar facilities, and telephone systems, special seats are available for the S class. There is wood paneling everywhere, not merely the fascia and steering wheel but also on large door interior trim areas; however, with the use of wood somewhat overdone, its up-market image tend to fade.

Koenig Specials

For the Munich-based Koenig Specials company, wheel dimensions present no problem. After the SL version, it is the S class for which Koenig Specials now offers an almost unlimited choice of wheel and body dimensions. The rear wheels are shod with 345/35 R 15 on thirteen-inch BBS rims. The front end has 285/40 R 15 tires on ten-inch rims. This "footprint widening" is feasible on limousines and SEC coupes. To accommodate the "rubber rollers," it is necessary to cut out the original fenders and to fit wide "chops." To this end, Koenig Specials provides distinctly offbeat fashioned fender extensions with well-rounded front and rear ends, the link piece between fenders terminating at the lateral bumper trim level. To meet this design feature, Koenig's in-house designer Vittorio Stosek had to rearrange the Testarossa "gills"—which he likes to use wherever possible—on a starkly fan-like pattern.

163

Konig: Mercedes SEC series (W 126).

Although the front spoiler, rocker panels, and rear skirt look chunky by contrast to the fender extensions, they still have a clean and smooth look. Conversely, the area where the rear fender extensions continue into the integrated rear spoiler of the trunk lid conveys a rather cluttered and fussy impression. For the limousine a pseudo-SEC hood is optionally available, and for all S-class models an enormous freestanding wing prominently positioned above the rear end. Koenig Specials will also modify car interiors to customers' specifications.

Koenig Specials can supply two power units, one a five-liter supercharged engine developing 213 kW (290 hp) at 4750/min and maximum 500 Nm at 3000/min torque, and the other a five-liter twin-turbo variant developing 295 kW (400 hp) at 4800/min and 590 Nm at 2950/min torque. With the two power units, acceleration from 0 to 100 km/h is between six and seven seconds, with estimated maximum speeds of 260 km/h and 270 km/h.

Kugok

The Stuttgart-based Kugok company came to specialize in S-class conversions, by virtue of its Middle East clientele. In addition to standard equipment, for example audio systems, the company's interior conversion range includes curtains, falcon-heads, bar facilities, gold-plated fittings, and other attractions for extrovert tastes.

The external appearance of cars has, however, received similar attention, with Kugok freely using glittering adornments to create the desired highly polished effect. There is a hood based on Mercedes 600 design, with real gold-leaf trim liberally applied—after all, money is no object—export-type headlamps, rear skirt with fitted number plate and red trim insert between rear lights, boomerang-styled TV aerial. Anyone who doesn't like all this ostentation is, of course, quite welcome to accessories of the more conventional kind.

Uncompromisingly discreet refinement is typical of Sport-Service Lorinser's work. The

164

◆ *Koenig Specials: Mercedes S-class (W 126), wide-body version.*

◆ *Kugok: Mercedes S class (W 126) with replica ex 600 hood complete with gold-leaf trim.*

Lorinser: Mercedes SEC series (W 126) with Lorinser rims.

conversion operation of the Daimler-Benz dealer, located near Stuttgart, was among the first to take an active interest in the products of the top-ranking local marque, with Lorinser from the outset being the originator of various styling features, some of which have meanwhile become production items. This speaks well for the bona fide background of Lorinser's conversion equipment designs, as exemplified in particular by the S-class rocker panels. Here, Lorinser has applied in up-market fashion the styling of the lower body side paneling, characterized by a narrow center section and flared front and rear ends.

The elegantly integrated lateral configuration has meanwhile become an accepted feature—perhaps somewhat toned down—of many production models, including the Mercedes 86 S class. Lorinser has matched the elegant rocker panels with a narrow rear skirt. A modified SEC hood is optionally available for

limousines only, unlike the typical Lorinser trunk lid and air dam, which is available for all S-class vehicles. The small lip fitted to the original hood underscores the sporty outline of the rear end, particularly on coupes.

Lorinser

As a novel feature Lorinser has introduced in-house-designed rims, available as single or three-part versions.

Finally, Lorinser has complemented the external conversions program by a traditionally broad-spectrum-based range of interior accessories. Apart from familiar fittings, for example, bird's-eye wood paneling, leather fittings, audio systems, and telephone facilities, Lorinser will also fit the Airclean equipment, incorporating a filter system. This facility is to protect the car's interior so far as possible from excess air pollution, particularly in snarled-up traffic situations, underpasses, and underground garages, and is available as an optional extra.

Schulz: Mercedes S class (W 126).

Schulz

Erich Schulz, conversion and extension specialist, can offer a standard spoiler program for the Daimler-Benz top range, comprising front spoiler, rocker panels, and rear skirts of typical Schulz design, the same program configuration also featured on other Mercedes series vehicles. Also available as optional extras are SEC-based hoods for limousines and trunk lids with air dam.

Schulz will, of course, carry out interior modifications at customers' request.

Trasco International

In line with its firmly held view that nothing could be improved mechanically, Trasco International has limited the scope of its activities to exterior cosmetic conversions. The Breman-based "facelift" specialist firm, with its financial administration in the Swiss canton Zug, is primarily interested in foreign customers, with special emphasis on the much-modified Mercedes S class. At the lowest conversion level, production cars are usually provided, modestly, with export-type headlamps and a front spoiler only. However, with the interior up-rated by the addition of wood, leather, catering facilities, telephone, and the like on a generous scale, the car not infrequently becomes the managing director's personal automobile.

Other Trasco specialities are discussed in the Cabrios and Special Bodywork sections.

Turbo-Motors

Engine specialists Turbo-Motors cater for S-class V-8 units, with five-liter production units being rejuvenated progressively in three performance-oriented stages: optionally available

Trasco: Mercedes S class (W 126).

Zender: Mercedes SEC series (W 126) wide-body version.

Zender: Station wagon on basic S-class design (W 126).

are 206 kW (280 hp), 221 kW (300 hp), and 323 kW (440 hp) power units.

Performance is boosted by means of two turbochargers that, on the 300 hp variants, raise maximum torque to 515 Nm at 1850/min, using pressure in the region of 0.4 bar. Maximum speed attainable with this version is a little over 240 km/h, acceleration from 0 to 100 km/h taking just under seven seconds. The 440 hp variant can do even better.

Zender

Germany's mega-conversion specialist, Zender, is similarly involved in S-class-oriented operations. The company caters for standard and wide-bodied versions, with fender extensions suitable for coupes only. The simple construction kit consists of front spoiler, rear skirt below bumper level, and rocker panels. Large trunk-lid-mounted rear spoilers and, where required, SEC-type hoods for limousines complement the range.

Wide-bodied versions can be provided with complete front spoiler and rear skirt bumper assemblies, plus elongated fender extensions with a rocker panel used as link piece. The rear spoiler mentioned above may also be attached.

For the S class there are Zender-designed five-star rims.

The Zender-owned Zender Exklusiv-Auto company specializes in interior conversions, for example, a station wagon version based on the 500 SE model, similar to the earlier ABC, Styling Garage, and GFG conversions. The superb elegance of the S-class station wagon version notwithstanding, it is unlikely to find a receptive market because station wagons or utility vehicles in this price bracket are rarely used for commercial purposes. For private use or an executive package, it lacks an image of its own.

So much, then, for S-class conversion specialists operating with conventional components, listed in alphabetical sequence.

Basically, these cosmetically oriented components could be fitted by any reputable workshop or experienced DIY enthusiasts. But there are also, and in particular with the S class, drastic operations combining potentially far-reaching interference with structure-strengthening body and chassis assemblies.

Nowhere in the world is there another vehicle type with anywhere near the number of cabrio conversion, body stretching, and special body options.

Finally, the exclusive use of S-class technology in a completely new skin is proving increasingly popular.

Cabrios

Conversions of works limousine bodywork to cabrio bodies has been carried out by special-

ist firms for quite some time. Even before the 1930's, the affluent owners of Mercedes, Horch, Duesenberg, Rolls-Royce, and similar luxury cars had acquired a taste for conversions, preferably by specialized craftsmen. The finished products more or less resembled the limousine originals, but there were also exceptions that owed little or nothing to original designs.

The most frequently fitted bodywork, in those days, was the cabriolet. As cars were normally four-seaters, the fitting of open bodies on the very rugged and rigid chassis frames presented no problem. Monocoque designs were not known at the time and, consequently, a massive foundation, that is, a chassis, was indispensable. After World War II, the long-established tradition of customized cabriolet bodywork continued as if nothing had happened.

Daimler-Benz was an exception because nearly all models were available as factory cabrios, but firms like Authenrieth, Baur, Kar-

Old Mercedes 300 S as three-seater cabrio (1951/52) with three-liter six-cylinder engine, output 150 hp.

Daimler-Benz cabrio based on Mercedes 220 SE design.

mann, Hebmuller, and Wendler knocked the tops off DKW's Sonderklasse, BMW's V-8 limousine, and the VW Beetle—with the latter being converted to an ostentatiously tearaway two-seater Hebmuller sports cabrio. In the 1960's, cabrio conversions became even more popular. Models like Ford's baroque-looking Variant and its successor, the 17M-Badewanne (Bathtub), Opel's Rekord, Chapron's Citroen DS, and others had their hard tops knocked off and soft tops fitted. It was the heyday of English roadsters like MG, Austin-Healey, Jaguar E, and Aston-Martin, also of the open-top Ferraris, Maseratis, Fiats, and Lancias, and last, but by no means least, BMW 507 and 503 cabrios and the Mercedes 190 SL, 230 SL, and 300 SL roadsters.

After World War II, Daimler-Benz also carried on the old works cabrio tradition, with the 170 V, 170 DS, 220 A, 300 Adenauer, and 300 S all optionally available ex-works as either limousine or cabrio versions. Fresh-air enthusiasts had the time of their lives! The follow-up models very largely put an end to this tradition.

In keeping with an increasingly safety-oriented philosophy and the need to increase productivity, mass production of cabrio versions was dispensed with. Whatever there was by way of cabrios comprised, as a rule, offshoots of coupe versions most likely to appeal to a clientele with more sophisticated tastes and fatter wallets.

With Daimler-Benz, for instance, the follow-up to the 170 cabrio version was neither the 180 nor 190 variant, but the 220 cabrio as an independent offshoot of the 220 limousine and 220 coupe variant, and, as an open roadster, the 190 SL sportscar. The 300 SL roadster also replaced the legendary gullwing 300 SL model.

The following Daimler-Benz generation retained the cabrio, based on the newly introduced S-class series. The 250 SE cabrio, later also available as 280 SE and 350 SE versions, was the legitimate successor of the 220 cabrio. Here too, the open variant was based on the coupe body shell, which was in design an independent unit, unlike the limousine. This series, however, bore a much closer external resemblance to the limousine and coupe/cabrio variants than its predecessor. The 190 SL was replaced, first by the 230 SL, then by the 250 SL and 280 SL versions, while the 300 SL model was abandoned without replacement.

When the S-class generation (W 116) was introduced in 1972, open Daimler-Benz model production ceased, with the exception of the SL series. American safety regulations, general lack of interest in cabrios, lightweight considerations, and cost-consciousness nearly put an end to the long tradition of one automotive species.

These were the days of oddly-shaped cabrios, Targas, roll bars, T-bar versions with two removable roof vents. The Beetle cabrio was replaced by the Golf model; and Porsche, much to the regret of fans, came up with the stopgap Targa. Then came the Triumph Stag, Fiat X 1/9, Datsun 240 Z, VW-Porsche 914, and US pseudo–sports cars galore—topless, but not quite, featuring little more than a sliding roof. At that time, Daimler's SL model was for cabrio fans a rare bright spot in a very drab world. Open air, no metal bits and pieces to obstruct the view of wide-open skies, an automotive dream come true.

Whenever there is a real demand for something—as there had been for cabrios for a long time—somebody is bound to turn up, sooner or later, to satisfy that demand. With the cabrios, it was the conversion specialists who turned up.

They pounced on a target clientele who would be expected to pay the hefty price of conversions from hard top to open cabrio out of the petty cash. Bearing in mind the ever-increasing popularity of the Mercedes S class with the wealthy, one could see a ready and potentially highly lucrative market for these exclusive commodities.

Far ahead of anybody else, Chris Hahn of Styling Garage (as it was then known) set to work with his cutting tools to take the Stuttgart craftsmen's work to pieces.

Firms like Schulz, GFG, Caruna, ABC, and bb Auto (formerly Buchmann) followed in the Styling Garage's footsteps. Koenig Specials (Munich) brought up the rear.

Since then, the cabrio family has grown. There are different versions, including four-door, four-seater cabrios based on limousine-style bodywork and two-door, 2+2 seater versions based on SEC coupe designs.

However, cabrio construction is not without problems. In the first place, the lack of a hard top must be compensated for by adequate rigidity. Secondly, the roof mechanism must be absolutely reliable, and that requirement is far from easy to meet because specialists capable of supplying a roof retraction mechanism likely to comply with the sophisticated specifications of today's clientele in respect of ease of operation, sealing, and fit are very difficult to find. In particular, with this class of big Mercedes cars, the conventional automatic opening and closing of the roof and a roof mechanism expected to function without hitch for prolonged periods is the beginning and end of cabrio construction. Furthermore, operating forces should be as limited as possible to enable the dimensions of electro-hydraulic regulating devices to be kept as small as possible and also to prevent excessive forces from acting on the roof linkage, with resultant danger to both linkage and roof.

This need to limit the forces is, however, balanced by the need to keep the top as taut and precisely-fitting as possible, an essential prerequisite for effective sealing and, above all, for minimum noise at higher speeds. And to prevent a cabrio top from looking like a hot air balloon when traveling at 180 or 200 km/h, it must have a very taut and accurate fit indeed.

Stiffening of the body is no mean task either. The limousine, suddenly minus top, should really be stiffened where it can't be done, namely at shoulder height, diagonally across the interior.

ABC: Cabrio on basic Mercedes SEC (W 126) design,
wide body.

Purely on theoretical/mathematical grounds, it is nearly impossible to provide for a cabrio the same stiffness as for a limousine without an enormous weight increase. However, the torsional resistance and rigidity of today's production cars is considerable; consequently, it is considered acceptable to attain torsional stiffness approaching that of a limousine at the cost of somewhat inferior road-holding and a rougher ride on uneven surfaces. Moreover, experience has shown that cabrios are not normally driven anywhere near as fast and as adventurously as limousines.

Whatever stiffening the conversion specialists provide will consequently be limited to reinforcing the floor side rails, the cross members behind the instrument panel and rear seats, spring mounts, window trim panel reinforcements, and small stiffening elements in the underbody and internal parts within the fender areas. The effectiveness of this method, even with low-profile tires and big, powerful cars, is proven by ABC's and Koenig Specials' overwidened SEC conversions—ABC offering, in addition to the standard two-door four-seater SEC cabrio, the coupe-associated wide-body variant. Tires fitted are 285/40 R 15 in front and 345/35 R 15 on the rear wheels.

ABC cabrios can be provided with the same interior and exterior cosmetic fitments as the fixed-top models. Top operation is electrohydraulic. Prices are quoted on request, but may be expected to range from 30,000 to 40,000 marks, as is normal in the trade for basic cabrio conversions.

Super conversion specialist Buchmann (bb Auto) came up with something quite unusual. His Magic Top SEC cabrio retains its original hard top—or, more precisely, what is left of it. To begin with, it is cut up, left, right, and center. The

Caruna: Cabrio on Mercedes S-class basic four-door version (W 126).

coupe roof is then removed up front and at trunk lid level. The rear roof supports, known as C-pillars, are similarly cut off from the upper half of the roof. Together with the rear window and its stiffening trim panel, they make up the second movable part.

To open the top, three electric motors first move the roof section backward until its front edge reaches the rear C-pillars. The freely movable top section will then be hanging over the trunk lid. When this position is reached, the C-pillars, together with the rear window and the roof section that is still adhering to it, slide downward in lateral body ducts. With the assembly in bottom position, the roof part will be located on a special trunk-lid-mounted holding fixture, the lateral ducts being closed by means of automatically operated cover plates. This electronically monitored operation takes about twenty seconds. Before one opens the top, the closed position of the trunk lid, the

open position of the locking devices, and the vehicle's speed (which should be under 50 km/h) need to be checked.

This toy is for the asking, but not for free. It will cost about 140,000 marks, roughly three or four times the price of a conventional conversion.

The Swiss Caruna company operates on much more conventional lines. It offers a cabrio version with traditionally restrained looks, based on the W 126 limousine design, and a T-bar Targa on SEC lines. The four-door limousine-based version will make any cabrio fan's day. With its long wheelbase, four doors, and steep-angle windscreen, complemented by a high-profile luggage facility extending a long way rearward, it recalls the golden era of cabrio motoring when open tops were not merely for the privileged would-be sports cars but also for more sedate four-door vehicles that took to the open roads, their lopped-off tops notwithstanding.

174

Their gentlemanly image earned them a limited edition chart.

These cabrios are not playthings of film stars, showbusiness personalities, motor racing stars, or champion athletes. They are chauffeur-driven, with elegantly dressed gentlemen and hat-adorned ladies occupying the rear seats. It is a good thing that these cabrios are still with us.

Caruna's SEC variant also follows unconventional lines; it has not been completely deprived of its hard top—only two roof sections have been cut out. The resultant layout is a Targa variant with central bar, known as T-bar Targa. Pukka cabrio fans will, of course, not be amused, but for others the additional fresh-air intake will be a source of satisfaction. Moreover, with increased rigidity and improved bad weather protection, the car scores over full cabrio designs.

For cabrio enjoyment on more traditional lines, based on SEC coupe design, GFG and Koenig Specials provide the needful, albeit on quite different lines. Whereas GFG relies on the original SEC body design, optionally incorporating spoilers, plus a cabrio top of rather more conventional design, Koenig Specials favors a thoroughly unconventional approach.

The Munich-based specialists placed a folding roof with million-dollar/sporty looks on top of the basic chassis, complete with Koenig extensions and shod with 285/40 R 15 (front) and 345/35 R 15 (rear) tires. With its flat, smooth, rearward sloping outline, the folding top would not disgrace a sports car. It all adds up to a giant superstructure of refined sporty design, whether with top open or closed. This Koenig SEC cabrio is a predictable show-stealer on the boulevards of the world's fashionable cities. The ostentation and extrovert image of the SEC cabrio notwithstanding, Vittorio Strosek, Koenig's designer, has succeeded in preventing the car's outrageously macho looks from becoming thoroughly tasteless.

Koenig's cabrio, based on Mercedes 560 SEC design, has a price tag in the region of 200,000 marks. With leather equipment and extra turbocharged push, the buyer will not get much change out of 250,000 marks. Whoever is prepared to foot a bill of that magnitude must either be someone hankering for a high-society image, complete with a Bentley, Rolls-Royce, or Aston Martin, naturally; or, alternatively, an extrovert wishing to project a macho image—by proxy, as it were, through a Ferrari Testarossa, GTO, Lamborghini Countach, or, while we are at it, one of these flamboyant superclass Daimlers.

The Strosek/Koenig SEC cabrio conversion probably stopped just short of the line separating what can still be sold in European countries from what cannot. All too frequently, the car is identified with its owner's personality, and it would really be a pity if a Koenig SEC cabrio had to be tucked away in a garage to be furtively taken for a spin under cover of darkness, lest the neighbors start hinting at one's keeping the wrong kind of company. However, the way the impressive car looks now, it can safely be parked, with its limited edition tag, anywhere in full view of the neighbors, to draw their envious looks and comment.

Erich Schulz's S-class-limousine-based four-door cabrio is of much more subdued design. Unlike the Caruna cabrio, it has few of the conservative features traditionally associated with an automobile for top executives, its flowing lines giving it a somewhat lower profile. It lacks the break in the central weather strip at rear door center level, which takes some getting used to, and the cabrio top folds quite flat and elegantly. The fabric cover barely interferes with the outline of the trunk lid.

Without fitted spoilers the car looks as if it had just rolled off the Daimler-Benz shop floor, discreetly elegant, but an eye-catcher for all that. In common with other firms' designs, Schulz' hood is electro-hydraulically operated.

Styling Garage, based in Pinneberg, near Hamburg (production has now shut down), had followed similar lines. Chris Hahn, who pioneered avant-garde designs for Daimler-Benz, was also one of the first to build S-class cabrios.

Since the company mostly built one-off editions for wealthy Arab clients, there was no standard production program (as other companies interpret that term). With hindsight, however, it is safe to assume that Styling Garage built

Koenig Specials: Cabrio on basic Mercedes SEC design (W 126).

Schulz: Cabrio on basic Mercedes S-class design (W 126), four-door variant.

GFG: Cabrio on basic Mercedes SEC design (W 126).

both two-door and four-door cabrios, all with electro-hydraulic top operation.

Only a small percentage of these cars, have, however, passed the official acceptance test (TUV), because they had been designed and built for countries where no such test authorities exist.

Special bodywork

The special bodywork types built on the basis of Daimler-Benz S-class designs can be divided into groups: extensions (Pullman), gullwing versions, pickups and similar versions, body shell assemblies.

Extensions

The extended (long wheelbase) versions, also known as Pullman cars, date from the time when, as in the case of the cabrio, large numbers of them were built for oil sheiks. Although the

forerunners of long-wheelbase cars of rather more conservative design had been available for years, even ex-works, the real boom only took off with the latter-day prestige automobiles.

Daimler-Benz, for instance, offered long-wheelbase versions of the phased-out series 200 to 280 E (W 123), ex-works, mainly for taxi firms, hotels, and airport services.

As a consequence of the dramatically boosted image, worldwide, of the new S class, the demand for extended designs also increased. The explosion was most likely triggered in-house. The appeal of the 500 SEL prestige factory version, 14 cm longer than the SE variant, was concurrently instrumental in creating the emotionally conditioned impression that the SEL model was superior to the SE; more length meant more prestige because it was more expensive. Therefore, the ultimate is the SEL and not the SE variant; q.e.d.

By the same token, why should then "longer than SEL" not mean also "better than SEL"? Since

177

▲ *ABC: Mercedes S class (W 126) as Pullman version.* ◆ *Duchatelet: Mercedes S class (W 126) as Pullman version.*

then, the number of different extension variants has exceeded all reasonable limits. There are long-wheelbase versions where 30, 60, 90, 150, and more recently even 200 cm have been added to the standard SEL works design. With the 60 cm extensions, two additional doors, numbers five and six are even fitted in certain cases.

The additional body section can be inserted either between the front and rear door sections or between the rear door and rear roof rail, the C-pillar. As with the cabrio configuration, the major technical problem with the stretched version is how to retain the original bodywork rigidity. This is more difficult with cabrios, because with extensions the load-bearing roof sections are retained and stiffening members remain between the doors. It goes without saying that with extensions there is a limit somewhere when genuine problems start to appear.

Wheelbase lengthening in excess of one meter, for instance, is certainly no longer a straightforward matter as regards either subsequent stiffening requirements or road-holding. In such cases, extensive intervention on the chassis frame is unavoidable in order to achieve approximately the original torsional stability, symptoms of the deteriorated condition being bumps and rough riding on uneven surfaces, and also difficult closing of jamming, ill-fitting doors.

Similarly, the chassis—in particular dampers and springs—should be adapted to changed conditions whenever significant extensions are made, first and foremost because substantial weight increase resulting from careful construction methods, particularly by more than 60 cm, is unavoidable. With significant lengthening of the wheelbase, the driver has to learn how to live with the trucklike handling of the car, because he will regularly collect a load of paving stones and other parts of curbs when cornering.

Furthermore, lengthening of the wheelbase will of necessity require lengthening of the exhaust system, brake lines, and, in particular, the drive shaft. Here, problems will arise one way or another, due to the fact that modern body-shell construction methods aim at a harmonious component configuration. This is why,

with the development at all times of new vehicle types, the entire gear train, comprising all assemblies connected with the body shell—engine, drive shaft, transmission, suspensions, and so on—is checked for sympathetic vibrations within the body shell and the floor assembly. Sympathetic vibrations are triggered by the natural vibration response of a body, in this case body shell and floor assembly. The generating forces comprise first, the gear train itself, primarily the drive shaft, and second, the uneven road surfaces transmitting vibration through the spring-suspended wheels and the suspensions themselves. In view of the fact that the thin-skinned minimum-weight body shells are highly resonance-responsive, engineers devote a great deal of effort to compensate, for instance, against vibration originating in the gear train area by appropriate mountings and damping facilities. It is, however, precisely this compensating effect that can be nullified by an extended or heavier drive shaft.

The resonant area, however, is extended not merely by using longer drive shafts but also by fitting more powerful engines into small body shells not originally designed for them, as for instance when a V-8 engine is fitted into the small Mercedes 190. Here it is difficult to avoid the impression that the engine is not running as smoothly as in the S-class package designed for it.

One of the firms offering Pullman variants based on big Mercedes limousine design is ABC. Its range comprises different extensions, including some with additional doors and a third seat row. The long-wheelbase versions can, however, also be fitted with all ABC extras for the interior and exterior of the car. There are spoiler kits for the outside and matching wood, leather, and audio facilities for the interior. The newly acquired additional space can optionally be used for other sophisticated accessories, for example, television, bar, video, and telephone.

Come to think of it—to consider extreme cases—it would no doubt also be possible to make provision for interesting hobbies, for example, model railroads, roulette, or one-armed bandits, in the newly created capability—

*Ronny Coach Building: Mercedes S class (W 126),
Pullman version, the Etoile.*

Trasco: Mercedes SEC series (W 126), Pullman version.

180

GFG: Mercedes S class (W 126), Pullman version.

or quite simply fit a couch instead of the conventional rear seats.

Duchatelet's Special Diamond is also on the long side, and what can be done with so much interior space is left to the owner's discretion. The Belgian conversion specialist has provided the ample space available with folding tables made of precious wood with pullout drawers for bottles and glasses. In addition there is a stereo system, television, video, and a mobile partition between the front seats and passenger interior space. Finally the up-rated vehicles can also be equipped with Duchatelet-designed bodywork kits.

Gerhard Feldeverts, GFG, has a similar comprehensive program. This safety reinforcements and extension specialist builds a wide range of Pullman versions. He frequently also modifies the S-class rear doors. This operation involves considerable additional work, which only few of his competitors would like to undertake. The car shown in the illustration has been stretched both between front and rear door areas and between the rear doors and the rear door upper panel supports. Without these modifications the door would look as if it had been moved far toward

the rear without any particular reason, and access to the rows of rear seats would be considerably more difficult.

The limit of wheelbase extensions seems to have been reached by Erich Schulz, whose Pullman version is no less than two meters longer than the standard model.

Now, who needs these long wheelbases and what is their purpose?

Schulz's first extra-long specimen was sold to an American dentist who had apparently been looking for something like an office on wheels for his affluent patients.

Another member of the long-wheelbase family is the Etoile, also known as Luxury 46, built by Ronny Coach Building, an SEL variant with a wheelbase some 115 cm longer than the basic dimension. The car can be provided with a third seat row and whatever luxury fitments are desired, for both the interior and the exterior.

Visually most attractive are probably the extensions built by Trasco. First, an impressive limousine-based stretched version with an intermediate section of unconventional design, featuring large-diameter struts blending into the

181

Schulz: Mercedes S class (W 126), Pullman version, then the longest wheelbase (two-meter extension) car available.

front door back panels, which will no doubt draw admiring glances from anyone with more esoteric tastes.

Then, as a more recent venture, a stunning new long-wheelbase version based on SEC coupe design, a break from that of its limousine predecessor. The newcomer is probably by far the most elegant of all the S-class extensions currently available. The wheelbase is lengthened by the insertion of a section between the doors and the rear side windows, and this configuration, together with the SEC nose and flat coupe rear, gives the car an unbelievably smooth and by no means ostentatious appearance.

Trasco deserves particular praise, because the SEC extension is one of the very few genuinely new ideas from which something concrete has emerged—and that is saying a lot in a trade that frequently enough owes its living to copying other people's bodywork and "borrowing" ideas.

In this context, reference should also be made to Chris Hahn, formerly of Styling Garage,

a well-known generator of new ideas. With his SEL-based Jumbo he went one step—or more precisely two steps—further with the extension concept by adding additional centimeters to the remaining two dimensions (width and height). His 600 SGS Royal version not merely had 60 cm added to its wheelbase, but concurrently 20 cm to the width and 5 cm to its height. The car carries a price tag starting at 350,000 marks. Chris Hahn referred to his Royal automobile, not entirely without reason, as the "illegitimate progeny" of the legendary Mercedes 600.

Gullwing versions

An entirely different species of conversions is the SEC-based gullwing range. The construction of extravagantly priced gullwing cars goes back to the 1950's and their legendary 300 SL sports cars, which epitomized the huge racing successes of Daimler-Benz roadster versions.

Although SL gullwing cars were built for

Trasco: Mercedes SEC series (W 126) gullwing version.

only a comparatively short time and were succeeded by the conventional 300 SL roadster with standard doors, the gullwing design is still recognized as a symbol of an up-and-coming successful automotive German generation.

Surprisingly enough, the gullwing concept did not regain favor with Mercedes until the present-day coupe. It is, however, reasonable to assume that there was not sufficient interest on the part of potential buyers, and that problems arising in connection with the external appearance and engineering parameters of the works variant did not justify the reinstatement of the gullwing design, not even on the SLC coupe.

Chris Hahn was one of the first to reconsider the problems of building gullwing versions based on SEC designs. The first prototypes still bore witness to the enormous technical difficulties caused by the removal of stiffening roof sections and the weight of the upward-swiveling doors. Considering the cost of conversions—in the

region of 35,000 to 50,000 marks—the least buyers could expect was as easy an access to the interior as before, the extra two doors notwithstanding. It will be appreciated that, with a low-profile coupe and limited headroom, with little margin for reinforcements in the roof area, this is quite a tall order. Moreover, provision must be made for the significant forces and momentum generated by the upward-tilted gullwing doors to be absorbed by the windshield trim panels and lateral supports (B-pillars) without adverse effect on front seat headroom or rear seat accessibility.

Conversely, stiffness is enhanced by the door-bottom side supports; in common with many sports cars, they can be considerably higher and reinforced, in keeping with the sporty image of the gullwing car. The doors, however, will not extend downward anywhere near as far as with the SEC variant, and access will become much more difficult. This is why some

▲ *Duchatelet: Mercedes SEC series (W 126) gullwing version.*   ▼ *Sbarro: Mercedes SEC series (W 126) gullwing version.*

gullwing conversion specialists dispense with the reinforced layout and retain the very low location of the bottom trim panel of the standard door version. These include GFG and Trasco; Franco Sbarro, the leading Swiss conversion specialist, prefers the variant incorporating extended side supports. Apart from the upward-tilting doors, generous provision of spoilers and fat tires, 285/40 R 15 (front) and 345/35 R 15 (rear), enhance the eye-catching appearance of the GFG gullwing car. Extended fenders accommodate the tires.

The Trasco Gullwing design is much more conservative. Since it dispenses with fender extensions, relatively narrow tires are quite adequate.

The most conspicuous feature of the Trasco design is the near-vertical end position of the upward-tilted doors.

Franco Sbarro and his partner, the Belgian conversion specialist Duchatelet, who is ob-

viously Sbarro's authorized distributor, place emphasis on more extensive cosmetic modifications on their gullwing car. Apart from the already mentioned high side supports, Sbarro has added to the cosmetic modifications of the SEC coupe by a wide circular grooved strip in the side sections and rear skirt, plus an apparently shortened rear with less overhang and a correspondingly forward-extended front section. A dramatically reshaped front grille, extending over the radiator and the headlamps, and a rear portion that has been placed at a higher level and given a flatter rear window combine to provide an esoteric visual image, unmatched by the production SEC coupe. Sbarro's specimen is complemented by fat tires under wide fender extensions, giving an added boost to the all-out sporty image.

This package is available from Sbarro under the name of either 500-Portes-Papillon-Gullwing or of Duchatelet's Albatross variant. However,

Kodiak: Gullwing coupe with optional S-class technology.

unless you can put the wherewithal, to the tune of a minimum of 250,000 marks, on the table, forget the gullwings. If, on the other hand, you have a little extra left, you might invest it in the Mercedes Sbarro sports version with a few niceties added like manual five-speed or, optionally, a 6.9-liter engine—also a 400 hp Bi-Turbo drive for good measure. Mind you, this will add a few marks to the bill—to be more precise, four zeros added.

The absolute limit with gullwing doors and, as most people will agree, with Daimler-Benz conversions in general, is represented by Franco Sbarro's Berlina Gullwing 4. This type identification is applied to a Mercedes 500 SEL named Berlina with gullwing doors multiplied by four, hence Gullwing 4. For this version, rear passengers can also enter the interior through doors tilted upward. This "fun" design has been a one-off happening, so far; it cost a mere 350,000 marks or thereabouts. The price includes completely modified doors, which are somewhat narrower than the original doors because space had to be found between the two gullwings on either side for the hydraulic cylinders needed for opening and closing the doors, and also for

wider central supports to restore the rigidity of the bodywork.

As an extra included in the price, there is the most powerful works V-8 engine ever built by Daimler-Benz since the War, with a capacity of 6.9 liters, originating from the last S-class series.

Pickups and similar versions

In the wake of the American pickup boom, Styling Garage built an SEC coupe-based vehicle for a wealthy Arab customer, which has remained a one-off venture. To meet the specification, Daimler's most expensive showpiece had to undergo major "surgery" on its rear portion: a utility body, complete with side panels, was transplanted, its wheelbase was drastically shortened, and the elegant wheels were replaced by massive off-road-type wheels with matching knobbly cross-country tires.

Bodyshell assemblies

What is no longer one-off, but is obviously the beginning of new Mercedes-Tunings activity, is a new range of cars based exclusively on in-house Daimler-Benz technology applications.

Styling Garage: Mercedes SEC series (W 126) pickup version.

This development has been brought about by the dramatic shift in business policies and the concomitant reorientation of the image of three-star-adorned power units toward the sporting aspects. Now, the prestigious four-cylinder sixteen-valve version, developed on Daimler's instructions by England's Formula 1 "supremo" Cosworth with the intention of uprating the image of Stuttgart's automobile engineers, is getting ready for battle. So is the powerful V-8 engine.

The Daimler eight-cylinder versions seem destined to replace the previously preferred V-8 units of US origin as limited-edition sports car engines. This is not altogether illogical, taking into account the fact that the capacity of the American "heavies" now rarely exceeds five liters, that the engines are outdated and project no technological image of their own, and that their reliability has now been matched, easily enough, by Daimler's V-8 engines. With the simultaneous steady upward trend of "offbeat" sports car prices continuing beyond the 100,000-mark limit, it has become necessary to boost the image of the power units by means of an appropriate advertising campaign. This is where the Stuttgart elite marque has done better than anybody else. The ability to provide Mercedes engines, transmissions, and suspensions is no doubt more prestige-boosting than a technically outdated American mass-produced V-8 engine plus a less-than-responsive transmission system.

With Eberhard Schulz's Leonberg-based Isdera company and Mlado Mitrovic's Kodiak company, located at Ostfildern, there is another important reason: both firms are only a few kilometers from the Daimler-Benz Stuttgart plant.

Eberhard Schulz, who at one time played a major role in Buchmann's (bb Auto) conceptualization of the verdicts rendered on the Daimler-Benz Mercedes C111 test car (car code name bb cw 311), reverted to the old idea after leaving Buchmann and setting up his own outfit; he now builds the Imperator 108i car in line with his own concept of the same basic idea. This vehicle, which owes much in design to the cw 311, is an embodiment of automotive superlatives concerning just about everything that is good,

expensive, and image-boosting. Access to the interior of the car recalls the gullwing doors of the SL series of long ago.

The output of the Daimler-Benz factory five-liter V-8 engine, 170 kW (231 hp), is adequate for nearly 250 km/h maximum speed and an acceleration from 0 to 100 km/h in a little over five seconds.

The transplanting of the new 5.6-liter Daimler-Benz unit, developing 200 kW (272 hp), into the Imperator is unlikely to cause any particular problem. Theoretically, it should be possible with this unit to attain about 280 km/h and an acceleration from 0 to 100 km/h in 4.5 to 5.0 seconds. The Mercedes engine drive is associated with a five-speed transmission.

Transmission of drive to the wheels is enhanced by tires type 285/40 R 15 (front) and 345/35 R 15 (rear) on 10x15 and 13x15 inch rims, respectively. Steering is on sports car lines—front and rear double wishbones, adjustable coil springs, and gas-filled dampers. The Imperator weighs approximately 1250 kg and has a width of 1835 mm, a length of merely 4220 mm, and a height of 1135 mm.

The price of the Imperator basic version is expected to be in the region of 175,000 marks—but there will hardly be anything doing under 200,000 marks. Lightweight versions and high-performance engines are also available against payment of an extra charge.

Mlado Mitrovic's Kodiak F 1 appears to be similar to the Isdera layout. This vehicle, too, is based on the original C 111 Mercedes design. It should be noted, however, that the Kodiak is not exclusively powered by Daimler's V-8 engine; it is mainly provided with US V-8 power units with 5.4-liter capacity, developing approximately 257 kW (350 hp). Performance and price are roughly the same as with the Imperator.

Peter Lorenz's ideas of Daimler-Benz's technology/fabric screen concept are something entirely different. The former Ford engineer goes flat out for the "topless" concept of the 1960's. Both his Silver Falcon and his Cobra are of uncompromisingly open design. While the Cobra is Lorenz's interpretation of the legendary AC Cobra 427 concept, the Silver Falcon is reminis-

Lorenz + Rankl: Silver Falcon with S-class technology.

cent of the Mercedes 300 SLR, with its long string of victories.

Lorenz provides both vehicles with an extremely rigid tubular frame chassis of his own design, which carries modified S-class wheel suspensions. Drive is currently ensured by means of Daimler's V-8 five-liter engine developing 170 kW (231 hp) as standard, which is always good enough for some 250 km/h. Before long, however, the new more powerful 5.6-liter V-8 units, developing up to 220 kW (272 hp), may be expected to ensure an even more powerful drive.

If Lorenz could be made to realize that there is no need for a roadster to do more than 220 km/h—it could not stand much more anyway—and fit a very short axle, then his Cobra version could continue the tradition of the original AC Cobra 427, with a seven-liter engine and its fan-

tastic acceleration. And with 100 km/h in four seconds from standstill, the sound barrier is not all that far away.

How about it?

The Silver Falcon is more mild-mannered. This eye-catcher brings back memories of the heady days when Daimler-Benz sports cars dominated the circuits; it has all the attributes of the classic vehicles of the 1950's and early 1960's. Lorenz himself admits that he deliberately adopted this style in deference to the great cars in whose image the Silver Falcon was designed. Taking into account the technological near-perfection of these sports cars, which really look like racers, concessionary prices must be ruled out: so, the two fast movers cost about 200,000 marks apiece. For parsimonious types there is, in fact, a roughly ten percent discounted Cobra version; the big spenders, on the other hand, have every chance to invest some 50,000 or

Sbarro: Mercedes 540 K replica with S-class technology.

100,000 marks in extras—possibly more, depending on the offbeat content of their requirements.

Franco Sbarro, leading Swiss conversion specialist, has quite different ideas again regarding Daimler-Benz-powered special designs. His discriminating clientele has a choice of two versions, both representing extreme trends; they are, however, diametrically opposed. One is a replica of the legendary Mercedes 540 K of the late 1930's and the other the avant-garde-styled Challenge supersports car. A more dramatic contrast of conversion designs would be difficult to find. While the 540 K version is as good a replica of the original classic German prewar touring/sports car as can be expected, the Challenge, by contrast, symbolizes ultra-modern pure sports car design trends.

The body shell, code-named by Sbarro "single volume body shell," has a rear section that is neither truncated nor aerodynamic; it terminates dramatically behind the rear wheels.

The hood abuts on the windscreen in a similarly abrupt way. The car is powered by an ex-Daimler 500 series engine, with twin turbochargers generating an output in the region of 257 kW (350 hp).

There is also, in addition to the first model, an uncompromisingly two-seater Challenge version, a companion 2+2 seat variant, which, unlike the two-seater, even has space to spare for a mini-trunk.

The 2+2 Challenge version is powered by a 3.3-liter Porsche turbo-engine, with twin chain drive transmission to the rear axle. The original two-seater Challenge version described above had a Mercedes engine with four-wheel drive.

When it comes to prices, Sbarro remains discreetly silent, since each car is built to individual specifications. Normally he will not even disclose his customers' names. Rumor has it that the price of a one-off two-seater Challenge with Mercedes Bi-Turbo engine and four-wheel drive was in the region of 500,000 to 600,000 marks. A 2+2 Challenge with Porsche turbo power unit and rear axle drive could therefore be expected to cost between 350,000 and 400,000 marks, subject to a minimum of three cars of this design having been built.

Sbarro's range also includes mini-versions of both the 2+2 Challenge and the 450 K replica for the little ones among the rich big ones. These mini-cars, costing between 35,000 and 45,000 marks, are fully working 2/3-scale replicas of the Sbarro originals. On the 2+2 Challenge, the roof has been thoughtfully removed to enable father to put junior's toy through its paces. The mini-Challenge is powered by a Honda 350-cc mini-engine, developing 27 kW (36 hp). It also features a speciality not found on the real thing: separate front and rear wheel braking for deliberately provoked wandering. Never too soon to put the racing stars of the future on the right track!

Chris Hahn also had a go at completely redesigning the SEC body shell. The outcome was the Arrow, without "Silver" or other prefix. It was built first as a fixed-top version and subsequently as an open cabriolet. More than any other body shell builder, Chris Hahn based his designs on the original metal skin configuration, major body shell sections being taken over, at least as regards their basic structure, from the SEC coupe, for example, windshield with trim panel, doors, and inner fenders. The front, on the other hand, was modified from scratch. However, with swiveling headlamps, the design still reveals its Daimler C 111 experimental concept which had been widely expected to become the 300 SL variant of the 1970's and 1980's.

The way things look at present, there is reason to expect the special-bodywork concept to be interpreted in many more ways in respect of the Daimler-Benz S-class cars. In this context, it will be interesting to see how the mechanical parts are used under a variety of fabric skins. If even more powerful four-valve/eight-cylinder or compressor-and-turbo units developing between 294 and 368 kW (400 to 500 hp) became available, sports cars with blown Daimler engines would break through the 300 km/h barrier and be capable of competing with the sports car elite, the likes of Ferrari GTO, the Lamborghini Countach, or the Porsche 959 for the best roadster's crown.

Classic SL

There is no mistaking the R 107 SL series' all-Mercedes origins. Long thought of as a flashy, pseudo-sporty type, the car, powered by a five-liter engine, now has the performance potential of a thoroughbred sports car. Even if AMG did race its 450 SL and, later, the lightweight five-liter 450 SL version (aluminium hood and doors)—the car never had what it takes to make it to the top of production saloon racing.

This could probably also be a reason why the SL series was never really considered Daimler-Benz's range-topping model—with the exception of a brief period when the SLC coupe did make it to the top. Indeed, it did not take the SEC coupe very long to topple it from its pedestal.

Nevertheless, the SL series can still count on the unswerving loyalty of its fans—to be expected, because the SL roadster is the only current open Mercedes model. Moreover, considered in an overall market context, it is one of the very few top-class cabrios completely lacking any visible integral top-support structure. If we add to these assets Daimler's proverbial high quality standards, the long waiting lists, comprising a worldwide clientele, come as no surprise.

Well-informed sources have given us to understand that the entire current SL-generation (R 107) output, preceding the introduction of the follow-up R 129 model, has, to all intents and purposes, already been sold out. Conservatively estimated, this is equivalent to some two to three years' output.

The Daimler clientele's lukewarm response to the SL series has been matched by the "don't really want to know" attitude of the conversion specialists. While there is at least something happening with the SEC coupe, the welcome extended to the SL series has been as warm as wintry sunshine. It will be interesting to see what

Styling Garage: Arrow C 11 on SEC base (W 126).

happens when the successor makes it debut.

This reticence could well be due to the fact that the conversion boom had barely taken off at the time the SL class made its debut; by the time that it was moving in top gear, the SEC coupe had already become Daimler's range-topper. Also, sports cars were by now getting on in life. They had, after all, been around since 1971 and were, therefore, also one of the oldest vehicle types. Anyone wishing to make this beautiful SL roadster even more beautiful, more exclusive, or perhaps even faster, will therefore not have the same choice as with limousines or SEC coupes.

Conversion firms

AMG offers a complete bodywork kit comprising front spoiler, rocker panels, and rear skirt. Available are also the familiar AMG five-star rims. AMG will, of course, also undertake conversion work on SL Models—not routinely, as on limousines, but more to customers' individual specifications.

With roadster or SL coupe conversions it is therefore advisable to consult company chief executive Hans-Warner Aufrecht and his staff in order to determine what is feasible at what expense and where the relevant blessing of the TUV might be needed.

The impressive wide-body ABC conversion, with rear wing and gold-plated radiator grille, speaks for itself. Like AMG, Brabus has an SL program, the scope of which is more limited than the limousine conversion schedule. Standard items supplied include front spoilers, rocker panels, and rear skirts, complemented by trunk lids with a trailing edge. The remaining items are for the most part on request, at least so far as engine tuning and interior conversions are concerned.

D + W and HF have SL programs on similar lines, limited in both cases to front spoilers, rocker panels, and rear skirts. Any work over and above the scope of these programs is carried out to individual specifications.

The HF kit, in line with other Mercedes series, again features the characteristic grooved trim around the body, similar to the first edition of the present-day S-class models.

Koenig Specials' SL roadster conversions follow entirely different and spectacular lines. The

Munich-based company is the only conversion specialist setup with a complete Mercedes sports car program.

Here again, in typical Koenig fashion, "full width equals maximum performance obtainable." Expressed in sober figures, this program reads 285/40 R 15 tires front, 345/35 R 15 tires rear, output 213 to 294 kW (290 to 400 hp), depending on the type of turbocharger (single or twin).

This output enables acceleration from 0 to 100 km/h in 5.5 to 6.5 seconds to be achieved, with maximum speed ranging from 250 to 280 km/h. These data are obviously in keeping with the highly aggressive and macho-oriented external appearance of Koenig's SL conversions.

By way of adornment, the car features an impressive front spoiler and bulbous wheel arch extensions with Testarossa ribs—not much left of the typical Mercedes decently conservative styling. The aggressive looks are further enhanced by the engine-mounted air hood and the enormous slab-like rear wing above the trunk lid. Anyone hankering for an "Aggro-SL version" will not be able to manage without Koenig's brainchild, provided, of course, that the odd 45,000 marks, perhaps plus a penny or two to cover the cost of the enhanced visual impact, present no problem.

Sportservice Lorinser operates on far more conservative lines. The conversion program, in addition to near-mandatory accessories like front spoilers, rocker panels, and rear skirts, comprises Lorinser's in-house-designed trailing-edge trunk lids and a unique SEC-style hood not available elsewhere. This feature is in keeping with Lorinser's principle: SL models should not conceal their SEC origins. For the former, Lorinser will also supply in-house-styled rims and, in common with AMG and others, will undertake interior restyling work.

Schulz Tuning and leading conversion specialist Zender have minimum conversion programs, with either firm including front spoilers, rocker panels, and rear skirts in its standard range. In an overall design context, Zender goes to considerable lengths to retain the discreet elegance of the original. Individualists wishing to distance themselves straightaway from the "hoi polloi" image of the production SL can avail themselves of Zender's twin circular headlamp sets.

With a firm like Schulz-Tuning, specializing in Daimler-Benz conversions, it is therefore reasonable to expect individual requirements for such things as interior conversions and engine tuning to be met. Even so, however, it would be advisable to establish beforehand whether the TUV will have any objections to whatever is planned.

Generally speaking, the conversion specialists' treatment of the SL series was rather low-key, with the notable exception of the Munich-based Koenigs Specials, who pulled out all the stops for its SL class conversions. It will be very interesting to see what the response to the new roadster star attraction will be. Perhaps it will succeed in toppling the SEC coupe from its top position in the Mercedes hierarchy, if only for a short time. Mercedes-Benz conversion specialists would then no doubt find ways and means to express their appreciation of this development by way of increased business activity.

However, Franco Sbarro pioneered a new trend by building a one-off version of the classic 300 SL roadster based on the existing 500 SL design to the specifications of a wealthy Asian client. With the new design, the combination of state-of-the-art technology, maximum comfort, and timeless elegance was realized at long last and, what is more, without any intention of producing an accurate replica.

Fundamentalists will more than likely have reservations about the windshield (which remained where it was) and the rear section bulge (which did not), but a little driving experience with a car like this should suffice to convince even the most conservative-minded that it would not be wise to disregard twenty years of technical progress.

So, here at least, the SL model has managed to carve a little niche for itself as a top conversion specialist's basic design.

Chapter 14

A forward look

Representing Daimler-Benz's long SL sports car tradition are (bottom) the 300 SL gullwing and the roadster
versions (1954–63) and (top, left to right) the 190 SL

(1955–63), 230-280 SL (1963–71), and a representative of
the present series, which has been in production since
1971, plus the current types 300 to 500 SL.

AMG: Mercedes SL class (R 107) with AMG rims.

The future trend of Mercedes-Benz conversions is likely to be influenced by the market situation and by the Daimler-Benz range available. There is, of course, the further factor of what the conversion specialists will make of it.

Customer profile

The market for Mercedes cars is largely conditioned into two groups. The first comprises those countries with a basically British motoring tradition, where vehicle testing and acceptance procedures, like technical specifications, are not subject to stringent regulations. As a result of this liberal policy, cars appeared that sported gull-wing doors, razor-edged, sickle-shaped aerials, enormous rear spoilers, and other accessories of a like kind. These designs found a receptive market, first and foremost in oil-producing countries worldwide, but also on islands in the Pacific.

The tabloid press contributed its share to this less-than-desirable development. As the press thrives on headlines, significant technological features tend to be played down for the benefit of more important news like "seven automobiles with identical specifications but with seven different shades of garish paintwork ordered by some oil sheikh from one or the other playboy conversion specialist." As an afterthought there could, with luck, also be a brief reference to the 2 or 3 million marks paid for this extravaganza.

There were reports about car designs that could only have been dreamed up by madmen, with science fiction fantasy and technological monstrosities predominating. Even reputable magazines carried front-page articles about Utopian vehicles capable of unheard-of speeds,

ABC: Mercedes SL class (R 107), wide-body version.

whose design owed more to science fiction than down-to-earth technology: totally devoid of any sense of purpose.

On the plus side, it is only fair to say in this context that quite a few motoring magazines unreservedly distanced themselves from this collective aberration.

Then there is the mentality of customers from the second group of countries: The system of mandatory technical commissioning procedures, adopted in Central European countries, alone prevents the development of components likely to involve a traffic hazard, because they will stand no chance of approval and would consequently meet with significant fail resistance for marketing larger quantities. Although it is true that there will always be firms that produce and distribute such unauthorized accessories, their operations tend to be short-lived, the public being soon informed that vehicles incorporating

such parts risk having their licenses withdrawn as a result of traffic checks.

Here again, the German Federal Republic (West Germany) has set an example that is now being followed by other countries, many components today being accepted without difficulty on production of a German TUV certificate. Many countries have meanwhile introduced acceptance regulations in line with German provisions or adapted their existing rules to the German ones. Subject to the technical specifications for car modifications and fitments being maintained and complied with as stringently as in Germany, any subsequent modifications on production versions or completely independent one-off designs should really give no cause for concern.

Although the cost of individual commissioning is prohibitive, there is, after all, nothing wrong with allowing such a one-off vehicle to be operated on public highways, provided the

🔺 *Brabus: Mercedes SL class (R 107).*   🔻 *D + W: Mercedes SL class (R 107).*

HF: Mercedes SL class (R 107).

technical specifications are complied with as strictly as with production models.

Apart from body-shell accessories like front spoilers, rear skirts, rocker panels, modified hoods and trunk lids, and the like, which nowadays are routinely covered by TUV certification by all bona fide conversion specialists, there are a few special fixtures much favored by prestige styling experts where official certification is not granted all that easily. For the most part, licensing of such way-out components for use on public roads is not possible at all or is so expensive that these products would price themselves out of the market. They include, among others, the enormous wings, shaped like trays, fitted 20 centimeters above the trunk lid, or "blown" engines. With their performance raised by means of turbochargers or compressors to twice the standard output, these engines would not stand the slightest chance of passing the exhaust and noise abatement tests.

With the decreasing market potential in "exotic" countries being compensated for by a clientele in areas like Japan, United States, Australia, United Kingdom, and Southern Europe, the importance of technical conversions on more conservative lines is increasing.

The limits of prestige conversions are widebody vehicles, provided that they are suitable for everyday use rather than for showcase applications. This, in turn, has implications in respect of costs, road-holding, and driving comfort. The main emphasis, however, will be placed on decently subdued elegance, in line with the old belief that it is the little extra touches that make all the difference.

With engine conversions, the trend is likely to be similar. There will be a few who require maximum performance within the limits determined by law, with considerable expenditure as an inevitable corollary. Others will be looking for increased performances within strict limits, without having adverse effects on everyday operations, but at the same time, making provi-

Koenig Specials: Mercedes SL class (R 107), wide-body version.

sion for a performance level noticeably above that of production engines. In the latter case, there would not even be anything in the way of conversions at a later stage in the event of the manufacturers themselves introducing more powerful versions. If, for instance, a 190 E 3.0 developing 132 kW (180 hp) goes into production, engine conversions with 2.3 and 2.6 liters respectively, and with equal output, would become redundant, but 3-liter units developing 154 kW (210 hp) would then be available.

Programs

In the course of the next few years, conversions will have to meet the following main requirements.
- advanced aerodynamics for technical stylists
- wide-body designs for prestige conversions
- everyday capability for conversions, with emphasis on conservative elegance

- TUV certification to accommodate high-performance-biased conversion specialists

Recent remarkable examples are the wind tunnel advertising projects of AMG, Brabus, and Lorinser, all originating from the new mid-range W 124. For some considerable time Brabus' advertising campaign was based on his self-established "C_d world record" for production limousines.

AMG similarly signaled two new projects as a challenge to the competition: the V-8 four-valve version, as avant-courier of a tentatively planned factory engine also with thirty-two valves, and a computer-controlled chassis (on which other major car manufacturers are also working and which can be expected with more than reasonable certainty to go into production—at least for the top range). At a more advanced stage, the fast-moving potential "king of the road," the W 124 with 5.6-liter V-8 four-

Schulz: Mercedes SL class (R 107).

valve engine, will eventually parade its 300 km/h on public roads.

These are the current highlights of leading conversion firms' programs, which should be regarded as standard in the next few years. It is interesting to note that they were originally intended to be applied to the S class. It is, however, much easier to realize the high-speed version with the aerodynamically more advanced latest Daimler-Benz model.

W 124

The W 124 version not only forms a better base for subsequent high-speed developments, due to the better C_d value resulting from its outer shell, but also, notwithstanding its lower grading in the model hierarchy, offers better prerequisites for good road-holding behavior at high and maximum speeds. Here there is no need for using brute engine power in order to

break the sound barrier; the required performance can be limited in elegant fashion by means of outstandingly efficient aerodynamics.

In terms of the S class, the W 124 required to reach the 300 km/h limit would, for the new mid-range models, have to develop something in the region of 380 kW (520 hp) instead of 265 kW (360 hp), provided that the factory data for the S-class top model are correct and that the drag coefficient and remaining operating parameters are not significantly changed in the course of conversion operations.

This means that the next conversion compressor or bi-turbo generation on a 5.6-liter engine basis, developing an estimated 367 kW (500 hp), will also get the S class near the sound barrier. It will do this only, as mentioned before, by the use of brute force, which will do the transmission, chassis, and usually also the service life and everyday convenience factors no good at all. Conversion specialists cannot normally have sufficient potential capability to be able to

199

replace all these power units with higher load-able ones, quite apart from the fact that components suitable for 500 hp outputs cannot be purchased over the counter. If they were available, they would originate from competition inventories or minimum-quantity batches, and it is doubtful whether they are as reliable and maintenance-friendly as the production units.

Conversely, the 5.6-liter mid-range Mercedes W 124, producing 265 kW (360 hp), could manage with a production transmission and S-class chassis parts, possibly with a few reinforcements if needed.

The market for the compact Mercedes 190 is very largely played out. In the absence of new plant-generated variants, it is difficult to see how anything genuinely novel could be launched.

The new mid-range W 124 series is representative of Daimler's most sophisticated state-of-the-art production range. It comprises quite a few former conversion parts. As good as certain are the prospects of marketing further high-speed versions, for example, AMG's extended versions, based on limousine designs and coupe design offshoots, mainly cabrios, perhaps even a gullwing model, all capable of maximum speeds approaching the 300 km/h mark.

As for S-class-based developments, here again there is very little constituting a new departure. In an overall engine context, the new in-plant-generated 5.6-liter unit will almost certainly bring about a dramatic output rise on advanced application cars, from 294 kW (400 hp) to 367 kW (500 hp).

Moreover, taking into account state-of-the-art engine and chassis technological developments, the three limousine variants may well be expected to become the basis for complete in-plant-assembled versions, particularly small-batch production sports cars.

Engine tuning operations frequently resort to mechanical, rather than turbocharging, systems because the former, in addition to being much less expensive, are much easier to operate and more reliable.

With the sports car SL series, extensive new developments can no longer be expected because before long it will have a successor, which is technologically in a leading position among its peers.

This will, in turn, open up for the top-ranking conversion specialists new vistas, the likes of which have never existed before. A similar comment very likely also applies to the follow-up model of the existing S class. Even at this stage, the conversion experts' twin mottos should be "Wait and see" and "Be prepared."

S-class W 140

Although there is not much of significance known about the new Daimler-Benz S-class series, designated W 140 for in-house purposes, there is every reason to believe it to be well on the way to becoming yet another "star of the three-star range."

However, what little information there is available will more than likely make the conversion specialists' day. So far as appearance is concerned, the new S-class bodywork concept is expected to have a visual impact undreamed of in the range-topping limousines. As with the Baby Benz and the new mid-range versions, at the very least the shape of things to come can be evaluated even at this stage—what restyling can do to the original discreetly restrained-looking production bodywork.

A lower chassis and wider rims, in conjunction with painted bumpers, are basically all that is needed for the wedge shape to become clearly visible.

Given the fitting of similar styling-oriented components, the overall image of the new S class can be expected to be similar to that of the two smaller limousines, but obviously far more impressive.

A similar, perhaps even stronger impression is likely to be created by the SEC coupe.

That the conversion specialists will take to cabrio and extension building is predictable, unless the Stuttgart management can see marketing prospects for in-house developments. Similarly practicable are gullwing coupes, probably four-wing variants on the lines of Franco Sbarro's Berlina Gullwing 4 design of the current S-class limousine basis; whatever smells of profit,

AMG: Front spoiler with automatic speed-controlled adjustment; shifts downward with increasing speed.

Brabus: Mercedes 230 E (W 124) conversion. 1985 wind-tunnel-tested 0.26 C_d was the production limousine best.

no matter how faintly, has a habit of turning up again, more often than not with minor modifications, someplace else in the trade.

There is also a potential market for Chris Hahn's "over-widened" limousine concept, a kind of super-Mercedes design.

Daimler-Benz is unlikely to launch a model with dimensions exceeding even those of the SEL limousine, and which might be considered a successor to the Mercedes 600, unless the twelve-cylinder super-engine were to be fitted to the new S-class cars. That would make it a range-topping model that even Daimler-Benz might consider a worthwhile proposition, always pro-vided the associated expenditure could be kept within reasonable limits and the traditional Daimler quality standards were not jeopardized.

In the event of the twelve-cylinder model going into production without any dedicated larger-size bodywork being available, the conversion specialists could have a go, with a fair chance of success, at competing for the laurels of builder of the best and widest body shell. Afterward, as in the case of the Styling Garage's Royale model, the works version can be extended along the three axes—in length, width, and height.

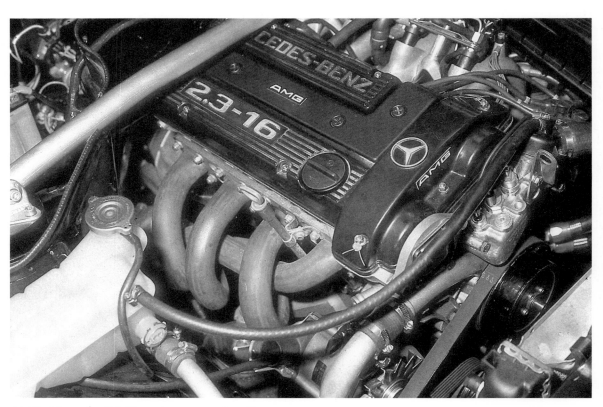

AMG: Mercedes 2.3-16 engine conversion (Category A-competition). Output 240+ hp at approximately 7500/min, maximum torque approximately 225 Nm at 6000/min estimated.

The outcome will be a "giant baby"—every bit as big as a Rolls-Royce limousine.

As for the new S-class versions, the show-case tuning specialists will no doubt put their money straightaway on wide-body variants with maximum dimension tires, that is 285/40 R 15 in front and 345/35 R 15 on the rear wheels, so that here there is no longer anything special.

Perhaps one of the tuning experts will one day fancy twin tires on rear wheels, for instance 205/50 R 16 or 225/50 R 16 twins and 345/35 R 15 in front. Then, with added four-wheel drive, ABS, and an engine output between 500 and 600 hp, the power available will no doubt be adequate enough for a 2½-meter-wide SEC version, weighing two tons without load and capable of accelerating without much difficulty to 100 or even 200 km/h, cruising at 260 km/h or more.

Trouble is that our roads are getting narrower and narrower. Rules and regulations applicable to heavy-goods vehicles must be obeyed, and this vehicle is more than two meters wide.

With the anticipated application of four-valve technology to all Daimler-Benz range-topping models of the different series, provision is made in-house not merely for built-in maximum performance but also for nearly ideal tuning prerequisites for performance boosting to levels that only a few years ago could be achieved by competition power units only. There is also obviously a Daimler-Benz managment-level ruling to the effect that production version maximum speeds should be limited in-plant to 250 km/h in order to prevent speeds from esclating, as is currently happening, since the consequence would be the reinstatement of mandatory speed limits.

As the potential capability for considerably higher maximum speeds exists, it would be desirable for an "on-paper" maximum speed also to be specified. The data would then indicate, for instance, that an S-class top model with four-valve V-8 engine or with a twelve-cylinder power unit would develop, for example, 265 kW (360 hp); this would be adequate for a maximum speed in the region of 280 km/h. These data would be based on performance details of the existing 5.6-liter engine and on an anticipated significant improvement of the C_d figure.

Taking into account the electronically-preset fuel cutoff at 250 km/h, the specification would then indicate that this particular model has an "on-paper" speed of 280 km/h. Even better, perhaps, would be a reference to the manufacturer's maximum permissible speed for a given model, which in this case could be 300 km/h.

This method would, for one thing, bring about a widening of the engine tuning specialist's activities. If the electronics could be reprogrammed to ensure an adequate injection fuel supply, the car could, on the basis of the above example, run 30 km/h faster—unless, of course, more sophisticated requirements were to add complications in the form of rev limiters, close-ratio gearing, or similar refinements, in which case the indicated on-paper maximum speed for a given vehicle would no longer be correct.

There would, however, be another side to the specification of an on-paper maximum speed permissible for a specific model, which would not meet with the tuner's unqualified approval: Such specifications would need to be backed by theoretical and/or empirical data, something that, taking into account the vast accumulated know-how of the big car manufacturers, would hardly present much of a problem. The TÜV, however, as licensing authority, could not disregard any output beyond existing limiting data because the latter would, almost inevitably, have been computed with its consent.

For engine tuning purposes, there would consequently be in most cases a preset limit where any kind of performance increase, reflected in maximum speeds, would have to be ruled out. The only way out would be to place emphasis on acceleration, particularly taking into account the fact that with the new S-class generation there would also be a need to transmit the gigantic engine starting power to the road surface by means of four-wheel drive.

SL (R 129)

What has been said with regard to the new S-class W 140 is similarly applicable to the new SL

New SL series (R 129) available earliest 1988, featuring extreme wedge shape and minimum C_d. Options available as extra are electrically retracting top and automatically operated extending roll bar. As coupe (author's impression) promising future tuning attraction!

New SL series (R 129) conversion (author's impression).

Old Daimler-Benz special Mercedes 600 with folding rear roof section. The wheelbase of this Pullman version was 70 cm longer than the standard.

series (R 129), because they would be provided with identical engine ranges.

So far as the external appearance of the new SL is concerned, it would once more be a genuine sports car with an international image, that is, a much less comfortable-looking cabrio with a no-nonsense V-8 engine like the existing roadster.

The body design immediately conveys a more aggressive image and also emphasizes the distinct wedge shape of the more recent Daimler-Benz generation ranges. To this should be added the combination of the very low front section and the—by comparison—high, short, and angular rear configuration. It will consequently not be difficult at all for the conversion specialists to arrive at a rather elegant but primarily sporty/aggressive overall image by emphasizing these styling features.

If another SLC coupe variant were to be built, it would obviously be a much more suitable basis for a gullwing model than the SEC coupe. After a thirty-year interval it would probably be the first genuine 300 SL successor with sporty looks, sporty chassis, and powerful engine.

Perhaps one or the other conversion specialist could—even before that comes to pass—give thought to whether it might not be possible to provide the fresh-air fans' model with a hard top in the form of gullwing doors, in case only one roadster with hard top was to be built, in order to somehow enable the 300 SL successor to emerge as a "phoenix from the ashes."

As with the Mercedes mid-range W 124, the conversion specialist firms can be expected to pounce on the new sports car. Here, as with the new S class, there will be two different trends: one discreetly unobtrusive and the other as wide-bodied as possible. There can be little doubt that many Mercedes conversion specialists will concentrate on both variants without delay in order to grab the entire market for cosmetically oriented conversions, if at all possible.

The technology-biased can be expected to make a bid for computer-controlled chassis systems, as in the case of the S class.

Performance can be expected to be better, taking into account the windshield area—smaller than on the S class—and the somewhat lower weight, with output remaining unchanged. Compared with the existing S class, the performance can possibly be expected to show an even greater improvement because of the significantly better C_d figure of the new SL version. With the new S class, however, this figure is likely to be very similar.

As for the engine, AMG will almost certainly be technologically well ahead of the competition before the factory four-valve car makes its debut. The other conversion firms will be able to make up for lost ground in performance only by means of turbochargers or mechanical compressors.

An SL gullwing car with computer-controlled chassis, as a discreetly elegant wide-bodied version, tire sizes 265 or 285/40 (rear) and 5.6-liter V-8 four-valve (AMG) engine, would therefore seem to be as far as the first SL conversion generation can be expected to go.

Further improvements of these superlatives will be the second generation's responsibility.

Mercedes Pullman 600 luxury interior, including, behind a glass partition, bar, two-way onboard telephone, radio, and folding auxiliary seats.

Conclusion

Only a few years ago, the Daimler-Benz conversion concept was considered something like reaching for the stars. Notwithstanding the incredulous shaking of heads at the time, the Daimler-Benz marque has meanwhile turned out to be a highly appropriate takeoff point for conversion business activities. It would be very difficult to find any other make where currently so many, so expensive, and so technologically sophisticated postproduction modifications are carried out as with Mercedes models.

It all started quite modestly. Daimler-Benz had seen fit to combine a powerful 6.3-liter engine with a relatively lightweight body shell; that was in 1969. And suddenly Daimler was wanted, wanted urgently on race tracks, notwithstanding the unfavorable circumstances prevailing at first; this limousine was expected to lug around some 1500 kilograms, possibly more, even in racing trim.

However, the dedicated Mercedes perfor-

Styling Garage: S-class limousine (W 126) stretched along the three axes.

mance fans would not take no for an answer. What they wanted was performance and victory. The man who wanted both as much as anybody else was AMG boss Hans-Werner Aufrecht.

It soon became evident that what was good enough on the racing tracks, where the Mercedes-Benz cars had not disgraced themselves, was equally suitable for roadster conversions.

The urge to do even better had to be satisfied.

And then something else happened: It became fashionable to emphasize one's personality by means of cosmetic touches in order to leave neighbors in no doubt that one was just a little different.

That was the start of cosmetic conversions,

not always primarily for a technological purpose but quite simply for the pleasure of doing something for the benefit of the cherished four-wheeler's image—without having to face immediate bankruptcy, and without making the car unsuitable for everyday use as a result of technical modifications.

The initially reluctant TUV's eventual approval of an ever-increasing number of modifications, together with the higher dollar rate of exchange and gushing oil billions boosting the building of cars of more-than-extrovert design, untried until then, helped the prestige conversion business blossom out on an unprecedented scale. Concurrently there was a temporary slackening of interest in engine tuning, due to more or less informed talk about the impending

Daimler-Benz: Mercedes test model C 111 with three-disc Wankel engine and gullwing doors.

introduction of speed limits and about catalyzers making speeds over 100 km/h no longer worth consideration.

When it was decided not to introduce any general speed limit after all, and when the well-documented evidence had become available that even modified engines could be very environment-friendly indeed, interest in performance up-rating was quickly revived.

Concurrently, the lower dollar rate of exchange, linked with the dollar-supported crude oil prices, caused the main markets for prestige tuning, that is, the Arab oil-producing countries and the United States, to collapse.

So it looks as if the "all-out-cosmetic con-version" specialists will have to let some air out of their overblown organizations; then automobile conversions can be expected to revert to their previous Europe-oriented style.

The trend in favor of postproduction modifications, with the emphasis on bona fide engineering considerations, solidly elegant exterior and interior sophistication, and—for a limited clientele—also wide-body versions, is likely to continue for quite some time.

So, if Daimler-Benz once again launches a new model, the likes of which the world has not seen before, "reaching for the stars" might not be the appropriate terminology. It has, after all, happened before and produced a winner.

Appendix

ABC
ABC-Exclusive Tuning Company
Sudstraße 110
5300 Bonn 2

AIR PRESS
Airpress Automobiltechnik
GmbH
Postfach 21 49
6078 Neu-Isenburg

AMG
AMG Motorenbau GmbH
Daimlerstraße 1
7151 Affalterbach

APAL
Automobile Apal S. A., 25,
Rue de la Fontaine
4570 Blegny, Belgium

ASS
ASS Aerodynamic Styling
Rontgenstraße 16
8047 Karlsfeld

BBS
Firma BBS
Postfach 47
7622 Schiltach

BENNY S-CAR
Technik + Design Team GmbH
Lohndorfer Straße 178
5650 Solingen-Aufderhohe

BICKEL
Bickel-Tuning GmbH
Hindenburgstraße 20
7597 Rheinau-Helmlingen

BRABUS
Brabus GmbH Mercedes-Tuning
Kirchhellener Straße 246
4250 Bottrop

BRINKMEYER
Brinkmeyer GmbH & Co.
Kunststoffe KG
Krechenhof 1
4952 Porta Westfalica

CAR DESIGN SCHACHT
Car Design Schacht
Taunnusstraße 31
8000 Munchen 40

CARLSSON
Carlsson Motorsport
Rehlinger Straße 14
6645 Beckingen

CARUNA
Carrosserie Caruna AG
Aspstraße 8
8957 Spreitenbach, Switzerland

D + W
D + W Auto, Sport + Zubehor
GmbH
Fritz-Reuter-Straße 64
4630 Bochum 6 (Wattenscheid)

DAIMLER-BENZ
Daimler-Benz AG
Mercedesstraße
7000 Stuttgart 60 (Unterturkheim)

DUCHATELET
Duchatelet S. A., 116
Rue de Liege
4500 Jupille (Liege), Belgium

ES
ES Autozubehor
Hozhausener Straße 42
8265 Neuotting

GEMBALLA
Gemballa Automobilinterieur
Boblinger Straße 11
7250 Leonberg

GFG
GFG Turbo Technik
G. Feldevert + Co.
Amelandsbruckenweg 93
4432 Gronau-Epe

HASLBECK
Haslbeck
Toginger Straße 156
8620 Muldorf

HF
HF Auto-Spezial-Service
Sprendlinger Landstraße 171
6050 Offenbach am Main 1

ISDERA
Isdera GmbH
Busnauer Straße 40
7250 Leonberg 7 (Warmbronn)

KAMEI
Kamei GmbH & Co. KG
Postfach 3580
6200 Wiesbaden 1

KODIAK
Speed + Sport GmbH
Postfach 412
7000 Stuttgart 1

KOENIG SPECIALS
Koenig Specials GmbH-Car
Tuning
Flossergasse 7
8000 Munchen 70

KONIG
Richard Konig
Talstraße 8
7141 Beilstein

KUGOK
Kugok GmbH
Kronenstraße 28
7000 Stuttgart 1

LORENZ + RANKL
Lorenz + Rankl GmbH + Co.
Fahrzeugbau
Postfach 1648
8190 Wolfratshausen

LORINSER (SPORTSERVICE LORINSER)
Autohaus Lorinser
Kleine Rote 2, 7050 Waiblingen
An der B 14, 7057 Winnenden

LOTEC
Lotec GmbH Kurt Lotterschmid
Staatsstraße 42
8208 Kolbermoor

MAE
MAE Automibilumbauten
Amerikastraße 26
7300 Esslingen

MTS
MTS GmbH
Postfach 2240
7056 Weinstadt-Endersbach

OETTINGER
OKRASA, Dipl.-Ing. Oettinger
GmbH & Co. KG
Max-Planck-Straße 36
6382 Friedrichsdorf

RONNY COACH
Ronny Coach Building Company
L'Etoile
Brugsesteenweg 211
8242 Roksem, Belgium

SBARRO
Atelier de Construction
Automobile Sbarro
1422 Les Tuilleries-de-Grandson,
Switzerland

SCHULZ
Schulz-Tuning
Pullenweg
4052 Korschenbroich 2

SKV
SKV-Styling
Fabrikstraße 1
6751 Schopp

TAIFUN
Taifun Vertriebs GmbH
Hanauer Landstraße 151-153
6000 Frankfurt 1

TRASCO
Trasco Export GmbH
Steindamm 38
2820 Bremen

TURBO-MOTORS
Turbo-Motors GmbH
Puderbacher Straße 8
5419 Urbach

VESTATEC
Vestatec Schwien & Korning
GmbH & Co. KG
Karlstraße 2
4353 Oer-Erkenschwick

ZENDER
Zender GmbH
Florinstraße/Industriegebiet
5403 Mulheim-Karlich

All the addresses are in West Germany, except
where otherwise indicated.

Index